Weathering the Storm

A Crisis Management Guide for Tourism Businesses

Mary Lynch

Weathering the Storm

A Crisis Management Guide for Tourism Businesses

Matador
9 De Montfort Mews
Leicester LE1 7FW, UK
Tel: (+44) 116 255 9311
Email: books@troubador.co.uk
Web: www.troubador.co.uk

ISBN 1 904744 63 X

Typesetting: Troubador Publishing Ltd, Leicester, UK
Printed and bound by The Cromwell Press Ltd

Matador is an imprint of Troubador Publishing Ltd

Contents

Foreword

This book came into being as a result of sitting on a plane and reflecting on three very turbulent years in the travel and tourism industry. It's not as if there had never been a crisis before, and there has been lots written on crisis management, so is there anything new to say? I came to the conclusion that there was.

As Chief Executive of the English Tourism Council, I was responsible for advising industry and government on the impact of the many unforeseen events that affected the travel and tourism industry from the year 2001 onwards. What I have written here is a distillation of the things I wish someone had been able to tell me at the start of 2001.

In February 2001, Foot and Mouth disease was found on a farm in the north of England. For those in the travel and tourism industry in the UK it was the start of a series of crises whose effects are still being felt around the world. While the outbreak of foot and mouth disease was almost exclusively a UK problem, it was followed by the terrible events of 11th September – which had a worldwide impact. The later bombs in Bali, Istanbul and Madrid, the outbreak of SARS and the war in the Gulf just reinforced the view that tourism in every country will have to deal with unexpected events.

On my travels I talked to many tourism professionals, and I came to the conclusion that there were many common issues that we all had to deal with, even though the nature of the crisis varied from country to country. I also concluded that there was a great need for calm analysis and simple checklists to get businesses through periods of great anxiety. I found many useful articles, but books on this subject tend to take a very academic view. My aim has been to write a simple guide with no academic pretensions.

The observations I make are personal and the descriptions of the way a crisis unfolds are based on my own experience. I am sure it is a good discipline to think about who might read this book. I believe it will be of most use to tourism officers' – those people who are actively involved in selling a destination rather than a single product, but I hope it may be of interest to a wider audience

The tourism industry has faced more challenges in the last few years than ever before. I certainly hope that this pattern will not be repeated, but unexpected events will occur and I hope that this book will help speed a recovery.

Mary Lynch
September 2004

CHAPTER 1
Introduction

Most books on crisis management start with a definition of the word 'crisis' – the Oxford dictionary definition is 'A time of danger or suspense.' I suppose it is useful to define terms, but in my view most people know when they are in the middle of a real crisis. In tourism some people do over-react to inconvenience, such as a train drivers' strike, and call it a crisis, but that is not what this book is about. All of the events of the last few years have been unexpected; they have had an impact on a wide, sometimes worldwide audience, they have disrupted normal life and have dented confidence in travel. They can all be described as crises, even though they have very different causes, but despite these differences, they all have similarities in how they unfold.

Sadly, an occasional occurrence in tourism is an accident such as a train or plane crash. For the people involved and the company concerned, this is a real crisis. This book does not try and address this type of situation specifically, as I felt that there is already a lot of good material that has been written on individual company crisis. My focus is on events that affect an area, country or region, and go beyond an individual company. Such events have a very broad impact, and require all elements of government and business to work together with an understanding of the part each can play.

The aim of this book is to describe, in simple terms, the characteristics of a crisis as it affects travel and tourism, and to equip individuals with an understanding of how their particular set of circumstances may play out using some general principles derived from looking at lots of different events around the world. Throughout the book there are references to patterns, stages and sequences of events. Some of these will apply to a particular crisis like a carbon copy, some will not fit at all.

This is not an academic thesis but a handbook, which is designed to provide easy reference points to people who may be feeling overwhelmed. It is a template to use or reject, to dip into or read at one sitting, and to illuminate and support your efforts to help your country or business cope with the unexpected.

Types of Crisis

A look back over the last 20 years shows how many unforeseen events have affected travel and tourism, and yet it maintains its inexorable growth as one of the world's biggest industries. The desire to travel is very strong, and the industry has demonstrated an amazing degree of resilience over the years. What companies and countries want to know when they are affected by some unforeseen event is how their particular circumstances compare with what has gone before. To try and answer this question, I found it useful to categorise different events. Table 1 opposite gives some examples of each category.

In the following chapters there are some thoughts on how each different category of event will be viewed by the travelling public, and how this will impact on business recovery.

Natural Disaster

Events like earthquakes, floods and hurricanes are naturally occurring, and are usually a feature of the geography of an area. It is usually the case that the local authorities in such areas have disaster strategies in place, and will implement plans to assist their citizens and get basic services restored. Such events are crisis events, often involve loss of life, and disrupt the normal functions of an area.

Table 1 Causes of crisis in tourism

Natural Disaster	Accident, Environmental or man made disaster	Political/Terrorism
San Francisco Earthquake	Mud slide in Thredbo Australia	Egypt – attacks on tourists
Floods in Prague	Algae bloom in Italy	Kashmir
Hurricane in Florida	Singapore smog	Israel
Bush fires in California	Severe Acute Respiratory Syndrome (SARS)	Northern Ireland
Forest fires in France	Foot & Mouth disease in UK	Coups in Fiji – 1987 & 2000
	Oil spill in Wales	Gulf war 1&2
		11 September 2001
		Bali/Istanbul/Madrid bombs
		Tamil Tigers, Sri Lanka

These events are very harrowing for the people concerned, and will take time to recover from. However, these events may well be better managed than other crises, as there is a structure for dealing with the disaster, and financial assistance is available from civil contingency funds or through insurance claims.

From a tourism point of view, the immediate impact on the travelling public is very similar to the response to other crisis events. The reaction is a mixture of sympathy for the people affected, interest in how the problem is being handled, and some concerns about future visits if the destination was a planned or possible location for a visit in the next 12 months.

From a tour operator's point of view, the immediate concerns will be for the safety of any staff and customers in the immediate area. Once these have been dealt with, an assessment will take place on the extent of the damage and its impact on whether the destination is safe in the immediate future. This assessment will be done in the light of advice from the local government and the view of insurers. If the destination cannot be offered, then an alternative will be proposed to customers or a refund will be offered.

The decision on when the area is deemed to be safe to return to is also more straightforward. While the government will be keen to get life back to normal, it will not take unnecessary risks. The final decision will also very much depend on the attitude of insurers. Once both these interests have given the all clear for business to return, then the process of reinstating the destination can start.

The most significant difference between this type of event and other crisis events described in this book is that, in the case of natural disasters, there is no blame attached to the event. Such occurrences can truly be described as 'Acts of God', and will generate enormous understanding and sympathy. This is very important when it comes to getting life back to normal, as potential tourists' perceptions of the destination will not have been damaged by the event. An example of this might be the floods in Prague in the winter of 2002–2003. For a short period there was widespread coverage of the impact of the floods on the historic buildings of Prague. Tourism was disrupted and business was affected in the short term. However, by the following winter, there was little sign of the impact and business was almost back to previously healthy levels. Part of the reason for this quick recovery is that the floods did not affect the long-term image of the destination. In other crisis situations, it is more likely that the event – and the management of the event – will have an impact on the image of the destination.

Accident, Environmental or Man Made Disaster

The grouping of these types of events has been done quite deliberately, as many crisis events are caused by a combination of all three factors. It is also quite common for the perception of a crisis to change as the reasons for the disaster become clear. So, events that start out being described as accidents will turn out to have been caused as a result of the deliberate intent of a person or persons. An example of this might be the forest fires in the south of France in 2003, or the bush fires in Australia in 2002.

The complexity of these events usually means that the news coverage will be prolonged as the possible causes or explanations are explored. There may well be a search for a person or organisation to blame, and there will be public questioning of the way in which the local area is managed. The coverage will also be prolonged if there is conflict between the local and national government on the management of the crisis. The final piece of exposure is likely to be the reporting of any public inquiry on the crisis, although this does not often command international attention.

All of this will have an impact on the perception of the destination and the management of any recovery activity. These crises do not usually have a clearly defined end point; it is much more likely that there will be a gradual decline in the crisis conditions. This makes it much harder to plan relaunch activity and to persuade a sceptical public that the problem really has been resolved. Suggestions for dealing with these challenges are included in each chapter.

Political/Terrorism

Terrorist acts are not new, and some tourist destinations, like Israel, have years of experience in managing their tourism industry against a backdrop of prolonged threats and incidents. In the 21st century, though, we are dealing with a new phenomenon, as evidenced by the events of 11th September 2001. The horror of that day has had a major psychological impact on travellers, especially American travellers. It has moved security issues to being 'top of mind' when people are considering a holiday, and it has had a practical impact as governments have tightened security procedures.

One of the complex messages that governments have been com-
municating about terrorism in the 21st century is that it is not
defined geographically. In the last 30 years we had come to
expect that when a group had a grievance with a government,
they would try to inflict damage on that government. This usually took place close to home, so that Irish terrorist acts were
mainly carried out in Britain or Ireland; Basque separatists
mainly struck in mainland Spain, etc. This is simplifying the situation, but in general a potential visitor to a country had some
understanding that there were problems and still chose to travel
despite these problems.

In our new world the threat is being described as global. The targets chosen by terrorists can be anywhere that citizens of many
countries congregate, and so, since 9/11, we have experienced
terrorism in Bali, Istanbul, Saudi Arabia, Kenya, Madrid, as well
as ongoing strife in places like Israel. For the fearful consumer
the perception may be that nowhere is safe, and therefore they
may choose to stay closer to home. For many consumers a decision to sacrifice their holiday and give up their freedom to travel is a decision they could not contemplate, but they will be looking for guidance. The challenge for those who are marketing in
this environment is to get inside the minds of customers and
understand what will give them confidence.

While the world has changed we can still learn from the experience of countries that have been through periods of civil distur-
bance or security threats to see how they rebuilt their business.
This is explored more fully in the chapter on Marketing.

The Common Threads

It is clear that there are many different occurrences that will give
rise to a crisis situation, and the nature of the crisis will make a
difference to the way the world responds. Even so, there are
common problems and challenges that will be faced, and a

recognisable pattern to the way in which the media, customers and governments will handle a crisis. Businesses involved in tourism can play a huge part in helping an area recover its economic health and confidence. They can also help themselves by understanding the path of a crisis, the steps to take to help their business survive, and the role they can play in working with government to mitigate the effects of any crisis. The following chapters are an attempt to help you do this more efficiently.

CHAPTER 2

The Path of a Crisis
A One Minute Version of the Book

This book is based on the view that every crisis passes through several stages. Each chapter takes a more detailed look at what actions are needed during each phase of a crisis. This chapter explains the timeline and gives a brief summary. If you are not inclined to plough through the whole book, then this is the chapter to read.

A crisis is essentially a period of uncertainty which is unexpected and has an unknown conclusion. In the very early stages it is worth knowing that there is a pattern that you can refer to which will help you to 'map' where you are and anticipate what comes next. Of course, every situation is different, and the awful thing about uncertainty is that it is uncertain. This chapter aims to give you a broad template and proposes that you think in terms of three significant stages. In terms of time, these are: the first three weeks, the next three months and the next three years.

Phase 1: The First Three Weeks

As we are adopting the view that this book is primarily aimed at coping with a generalised or global development, it is not necessarily the case that an individual business or country will realise that their business will be affected by an event. The early reports of a respiratory disease in one part of China probably did not ring alarm bells for the tourism industry in most countries. The first few days' reports on the outbreak of Foot and Mouth Disease in the UK generated some concern, but this was seen primarily as a problem for farming and agriculture. In both these cases, a measure taken as a reaction to the problem was the trigger for an impact on tourism. In the case of Foot and Mouth Disease (FMD), the decision to close all footpaths to prevent the spread of the disease had the effect of closing the countryside to tourists. In the case of SARS, the travel advice given by governments and the World Health Organisation made customers and airlines change their plans.

In this early period, there will be conflicting views about how serious any external event might be. There will also be many proponents of the 'It will all be over by Christmas' school. This phrase became famous in 1914, as it was the received view about the length of the First World War. The war went on for four years, and it is a salutary reminder that in the beginning we just don't know how long a problem will last. This is covered in more detail in Chapter 9, but as a general rule it is worth planning for a pessimistic outcome and be prepared to react quickly when conditions change.

At some point it will be clear that a single development (e.g. September 11th), or a combination of events is going to have a major impact on business. This realisation will generate enormous demands for information. The media, the government and the tourism industry will all want analysis, advice and action. What are the sensible things to do in these circumstances?

Actions during Phase 1

☞   *Organise your resources*: this means setting up a dedicated person or team to manage the problem. It is highly desirable to have a separation of responsibilities to ensure that at least one person is looking at medium- and long-term developments, and this is separate from the short-term response. What you know for sure is that the crisis will end at some point. You will need to be ready for this, and you need to get someone looking at this without the distractions of the here and now.

☞ *Organise your media messages*: this is covered in more detail in Chapter 6. As a minimum you need to prepare a brief description of the problem for the industry globally, an easy to understand view on the financial impact, e.g. 'This is going to cost tourism £100m per week', and an answer to the question, 'What do you think should be done?'

☞ *Review all the statistical information available*: this is crucial, and should form the basis for your communication with government, the media and the industry. A quick look at trend information, early feedback from 'barometer' businesses and your understanding of your own market will enable you to make some predictions. At a national level, the tourist board will be doing this exercise, and this can be a useful reference point. Many crises have a localised impact, so it is important to be confident in your own judgement if you feel there are good reasons why your area may buck the trend.

☞ *Set up a mechanism for communications within the tourism industry*. It is highly likely that there are already groups in existence that meet to network and share information. What you will need to find is a way to feed these networks with fast, relevant information. Email is the obvious tool, but don't overlook the 10–50% of tourism businesses (depending on which country you are in) which don't use email. You will need feedback and input from these businesses, so you must be able to receive responses.

☞ *Do some scenario planning*: this sounds more complex than it needs to be. If you can afford it you will find there are many consultancy companies who will do a detailed exercise that models a variety of outcomes and looks at the financial implications of each. In the very short-term you may not have the time or the resource for this. It is still worthwhile to get a few sensible people together and give them the challenge of answering a series of 'What if?' questions. They can also make some general estimates of the likely financial implications. This can be used (with caution) to get people thinking flexibly. Be prepared for the fact that your finance manager is likely to be uncomfortable with broad estimates and will want more precision. A more considered and precise version of scenario planning can be done in Phase 2.

☞ *Communicate with the customer*: the customers' reaction will be shaped by many influences, and this is covered in Chapter 7. What you must do is keep faith with your current and future customers. You will need to think quickly about cancellation policy, refunds, postponements or substitution. All the evidence is that business does return eventually, so you will need to think about how to protect goodwill while staying solvent.

☞ *Draw up your wish list*: in this period of initial shock, the media and the government are at their most receptive. This means that you only have a limited window to clearly state what it is that would most help your business/the industry to recover and flourish. If all parties can unite around a few key things and articulate these consistently, then the chances of persuading those responsible are greatly increased.

☞ *Review your existing business plan*: few businesses or tourist boards have spare resources, and therefore you need to identify what can be postponed or cancelled to free up time and money to deal with a crisis. Some decisions will be easy. For example, it is highly likely that spending on promotion will be postponed in the short-term. Investment or development projects may need to be rescheduled, and non-essential work put on hold. It is important that this is done to increase the flexibility of the organisation to enable it to respond at a later date. There will come a time when you will need to spend more, so this is essentially a rephasing exercise. Once in Phase 2 you may decide that some projects cannot proceed because the crisis is lasting longer than you first expected. This is not the sort of decision you should take in the first few weeks.

The end of Phase 1

These few weeks are likely to be a period of frenetic activity. Few crises are considerate enough to arrive when you have a clear diary. There will be significant demands from the media and others to play an external role, and the need for reassurance from your employees that the business – and their jobs – will be safe. Most individuals recognise when an issue is really serious and will give their time generously. During this first phase it is likely that everyone will work long hours and be very focussed. Be warned! This is not an option for Phase 2, as individuals will experience burn out and will come to resent the extraordinary demands made on them. In thinking about Phase 2, a key issue is planning resources to ensure you have enough people available to sustain the business.

Phase 2: The Next Three Months

In phase 2 the organisation or industry will still be in crisis mode, but certain new realities will have influenced everyone's thinking. There are several characteristics of this phase, and this section highlights those that are most common. This is not exclusive or prescriptive. You may well find you will experience more or less of these.

Media restlessness

By the end of stage 1 the media will have exhausted all of the obvious story lines and will have become bored – or moved on – to another news story. Chapter 6 explores this issue in more detail. The key decision to make is whether you want continuing media coverage or not. In some instances, it may be felt that media coverage will keep the industry's problems at the top of the government agenda – and so it is to be encouraged. In other cases, the view may be that a daily diet of crisis stories is bad for consumer confidence and future business. In this case, the role of PR is to keep stories out of the media. A good PR person can do either of these, but not both! In my experience, there will not be a unanimous view from within the industry about media coverage, and some skilful negotiation will be required to ensure that any internal disagreements remain internal.

Impact information

An individual business should have a good handle on how their business has been affected in the short term. The willingness of businesses to share this information cannot be taken for granted. Many commercial organisations are wary of releasing information which may help their competitors, or affect their share price. To arrive at a view on the scale of impact for a region, city or country is more complex. Few countries in the world are able to measure their tourism expenditure on a weekly basis, and yet fast delivery of information is what is demanded by government. The joys of measurement are covered in Chapter 4. What you will need to do is to have some measurement system – however imperfect – to provide tracking of what is going on and to give you an early warning of the first signs of business recovery.

Consumer attitudes

By phase 2 consumers will have formed some views about the significance of this crisis in relation to their personal plans. Chapter 7 explores this in more detail. The priority during this period is to provide good quality information coupled with reassurance. At some point the balance will shift, so that the focus moves to encouraging customers to travel again. The best way to understand when this moment has come is to commission consumer tracking research on a regular basis. My view is that consumers who were potential customers *for this period of time* will move out of the paralysis stage faster than others. This is simply because they cannot put their plans on hold indefinitely. If the crisis is still very real, then the priority has to be to encourage customers to postpone their visit. (A delayed visit is better than no visit at all – even if it does not help the cashflow position in the short term.)

Promotion and advertising

During this three month period there will be an urgent need to get customers travelling again, coupled with a desire to avoid wasting money by running promotions before the consumer is ready to receive the message. Chapter 8 explores the marketing issues and the vexed question of timing. This phase is all about tactical marketing to make sales and rebuild confidence. One of the early dilemmas is whether to go down the price-cutting route or the added value route. The Irish low cost carrier, Ryanair, demonstrated very convincingly that there is always a market if the price is low enough. In the aftermath of September 11, Ryanair went to the market with 500,000 airline seats to and from Europe priced at £10 and kept their planes full. Two years on, the impact of that decision on Ryanair's pricing policy is still being felt.

An equally important job to be done is confidence building. Therefore, short 'taster breaks' or day trips should be part of the agenda to get customers travelling again.

Government and public bodies

Chapter 5 explores the many ways in which local and national government can aid recovery. The three areas that are essential to focus on in Phase 2 are:

1. Making the case for financial support.

2. Lobbying for other measures which will help
    businesses with their cash flow, e.g. deferral of tax
    payments.

3. Providing good quality information to policy
    makers on how the crisis is developing.

The end of Phase 2

If you are lucky, there will be a milestone during these three
months when the crisis can be said to be over. (The oil has been
cleaned from the beach, the travel restrictions have been with-
drawn, etc.) Of course, you will know that this is just the start of
the long haul back to something like normal business conditions.
In many cases, there will not be a milestone to point to, just a
gradual return over a long period of time as confidence builds.
If there is no clear cut event that marks the end of phase 2, you
will know that you have moved to the next phase when you feel
confident about running promotions campaigns which are
about the place rather than the crisis.

Phase 3: The Next Three Years

The received wisdom is that it takes three years to get a business
or destination back to where it would have been before the crisis hit. This is rather simplistic – and Chapters 9 and 10 explore
a more detailed analysis of what 'recovery' means. Most countries and businesses are changed by a major crisis, so it is probably better to think in terms of adjusting to the new world rather
than going back to an old world order. This section explores the
major characteristics of each of the three years, and it has to
be superficial. Business is dynamic, and no-one assumes that
the world will stay the same. Since the year 2000 the tourism

industry has had a series of crises to cope with. In a sense, it has felt like the industry never got beyond year 1 of any crisis, because 'recovery' was hampered by the impact of the next trauma. Looking objectively, it can be seen that not all aspects of business are affected equally by any crisis. The likelihood is that there will be several timelines running, with parts of a country in recovery mode and parts still in shock. For the sake of simplicity, I have described them as if they were discrete.

Year 1

Winding Down the Crisis Team
One of the important judgements to make is when to close down any special crisis activity, e.g. hotlines, websites, etc. A total close down of support services runs the risk of drawing negative media attention, and may generate bad publicity. Crisis services should not be offered for an extended period, and a phased reduction of services and less regular meetings is a better way to ease back into the hard slog of winning back customers.

When it comes to winding down your crisis team, you should be prepared for the fact that working with the adrenalin flow generated by crisis can be addictive for some people, and they may find it hard to adjust back to more routine work. Their performance may drop or sickness levels will rise.

Learning Lessons
Chapter 10 reviews what has been learned by the industry. Taking the opportunity to reflect is very important. A business under stress is a place where a great deal can be learned. All sorts of weaknesses will become apparent and they need to be described and prioritised before the status quo returns.

If there are system problems they will be seen much more clearly and everyone has the opportunity to see why a lack of care, or lack of investment in the past is hampering business growth and flexibility. It may be that the organisation will decide to do

some things differently in the future and will import some of the
crisis practices into its normal business operations.

Promotions

Flexibility is the most important issue in this first year. A good
understanding of who your potential customers might be is the
place to start. It is quite likely that some of your source markets
will be new to you, and you will need to learn how to reach
them. For example, in the aftermath of September 11, the lack
of overseas visitors to London prompted London to look to
London residents as a source market. If you have been able to
protect resources then you will be running some kind of 'Open
for Business' or welcome back campaign. While this is a short-
term response, you must protect your long-term brand and
market positioning. Examples of such campaigns are described
in Chapter 8.

The Return of the Customer

Most people express surprise at how quickly customers come
back. After the SARS outbreak, Hong Kong was reporting 60%
hotel occupancy by July 2003, when it had been down at 15%
in April 2003. To an extent, publicity of any sort is good for
business. Any country or area, which has been 'closed', will
benefit from pent up demand in the short term. This is good
news, but should be treated with caution and the champagne
should be kept on ice. Winning back customers confidence is a
long haul.

Year 2

Winning Back Your Traditional Customers

If no other crises have intervened, the focus of year 2 should be
to try and have a real recovery built on the strength of your loyal
customer base who take their postponed visit, and the business
you win from new customers who were not previously aware of
what you had to offer. The flexibility that you adopted in your
marketing in year 1 may also have generated new packages or
partnerships which you can develop in year 2.

Tracking the Impact on the Industry
There is a real possibility that year 2 will be a 'bounce back' year, but it is worth remembering that the comparison with year 1 may well mislead. If you take year 1 as your base for comparison, then your growth figures are bound to look impressive. It is a good discipline to take an earlier year or an average of three earlier years to track how the business is really doing. Chapter 4 looks at measuring impact. Statistics will confess to anything if you interrogate them hard enough, so it is worth being clear about how you are going to measure success. If you have responsibility for tourism policy or the health of the industry, then there are other indicators which should be tracked. These include business failures, employment growth in tourism, and investment.

Implementing the System Changes
By the end of year 1 you will have a wish list of changes you would like to see in the business. This is the year to make it happen. The memory of the frustration you felt when you could not get things done will fade. Seize the day or complacency will be your enemy. This is also the period when your employees will remember the crisis, and will understand why some things need to be done differently. It is much better to work with this understanding than to let the memory fade.

Nurture Your New Relationships
A crisis brings you into contact with a wide range of new contacts – especially in the media. If you can manage it, these should be integrated into your contacts database and followed up at least once a year. Anyone who has been especially helpful should get special recognition.

Year 3

The Impact on Quality
In the best case, your customers are now back and business has returned to previous levels. You may also have improved the systems in the business from the lessons you learned during the

crisis. It is quite likely that some will feel that the crisis was not all bad, as it has removed complacency and injected a new understanding of tourism on the part of government. A question to reflect on in year 3 is what impact there has been on the quality of the product. A natural reaction of any business in a bad year is to cut investment or refurbishment. If this expenditure has not been reinstated, then quality will suffer. Visitor satisfaction surveys are important every year, but special attention should be paid to them after a crisis.

Uncertainty
The greatest challenge of seeing an organisation or country through a crisis is coping with uncertainty in a sure-footed way. These skills are very valuable as the real world is made up of the unexpected – it's just that the really unexpected gets called a crisis. You will learn an enormous amount from living through a crisis. A positive approach will give confidence to your customers and your staff and help speed a recovery.

CHAPTER 3

Speaking with One Voice
Communicating with the Industry

A Fragmented Industry

Everywhere in the world tourism experts solemnly describe their tourism industry as 'fragmented' and wait for the listener to be impressed. It isn't that much of a novelty, but it does partly explain why the industry struggles during a crisis. An industry with few players, like shipbuilding, will be very competitive when it comes to bidding for business, but will be able to reach a consensus quite quickly if there are threats to the success of the industry as a whole. The fact that there are a small number of influential companies means that each one speaks with authority and it is easier to build a consensus to allow them to 'speak with one voice'.

Tourism isn't really an industry, it is a sector, which includes hotels, surface transport, airlines, visitor attractions, caravans, cottages, catering and entertainment, to name just a few. It would be extraordinary if all of these parts of the whole were equally affected by a crisis. And yet governments and the media want a single and simple view of what is happening and what the industry thinks about it.

Faced with this dilemma, you have a choice – do you resist this expectation and try to explain the complexities of the industry, or do you respond to their need for the big picture, headlines and soundbites? In my view there really isn't a choice. In a crisis you need friends in high places and the media on your side, so you will need to find a way to represent the industry in terms that are clear and coherent. This is a struggle, and I am not sure that there is a country in the world that feels they succeed fully. This section describes some of the methods that have been used to bring the industry together, keep people informed and collect feedback during a crisis.

Sharing Information

Tourism is a service industry made up of many small players and this means that there are many specialist representative associations. There will be groupings based on geography (e.g. NYC & Company for New York), groupings based on type of business (e.g. the Caravan Club) and groupings based on business networks (e.g. Chambers of Commerce). Your objective is to give and receive good quality information simply and quickly. Your challenge is to do so at speed and to avoid duplication. There is nothing more frustrating for a business owner than receiving several different questionnaires from different organisations all asking how bad things are.

Sending Information Out

In the past, communication followed a common model of information being held at the top of a structure and being 'cascaded down' through an organisation or system. The world wide web has changed all that. Good communication really is about the power of using networks effectively. To do this, you have to abandon some concepts, like the idea that you own or control information. Information is the lubricant that helps the industry to function, to react and respond quickly. During a crisis there will be lots of information – much of which will appear to be contradictory. The important decision that you need to make about your crisis is which organisation is going to take the lead role in coordination. This means taking responsibility for 'telling the story', briefing the industry, interpreting the information, collating it and distributing it. In some countries, the answer to this question may be obvious, as the national tourist board automatically takes on this role, but a good trade association or government tourism department may do it.

It is quite common for this to be a sensitive decision, as people feel, quite rightly, that they know their segment of the tourism business better than anyone else. An Association representing small bed and breakfast businesses may not be comfortable if the spokesman for the industry works for a global hotel chain. To make this less sensitive it is worth thinking of this job as the creation of a hub which supports the other information networks. What you need to establish is the point where collation of information takes place. Your objective then is to feed this information into as many other networks as possible, as quickly as possible. This allows each part of the industry to tailor information so that it is relevant to that constituent group.

The establishment of a communications centre and the question of key messages is explored more fully in Chapter 6. A single point of co ordination is the best option, and this single point can deal with both trade and media issues. The way the information is used for the trade and media should be very different.

Communication Tools

The fact that the tourism industry is so disparate means that you cannot assume that everyone has access to the latest communications technology. You will need to plan for communication using all methods, including paper based methods like newsletters. The challenge is to strike the right balance between getting fast information to those who are on line and getting relevant information that is not out of date to those who are off line. This is where the idea of a network of networks becomes very important. At the start of the crisis you need to be inclusive and ensure that every trade association or industry body knows that fast information is critical and that the aim is to work together.

It may be helpful to think of the 'Six degrees of separation' model. This suggests that you can connect any two people in the world in six steps. If you apply this idea within your tourism industry, you can see that it is possible to get a message to thousands of businesses as long as you use all the formal and informal networks that exist.

You do need to decide on a primary vehicle for your briefing and this will almost certainly be electronic. In the early stages of a crisis you may want to establish a daily briefing and revert to weekly updates as a pattern emerges. In England during the foot and mouth crisis, the feedback was that a daily briefing was useful to start with. The situation was changing very quickly and business operators scanned it each day for an update. When you are planning the frequency of such a briefing do not underestimate the level of resource you will need to do this.

Essential Briefing Topics

What most businesses have in common during a crisis is fear. The fear comes from the fact that there are many unanswered questions which lead people to worry about the future. The hoped for promotion, their savings or their livelihood may be at risk. You cannot predict the future, but you can help businesses to get a sense of what is going on and what they can do about it. Some topics are suggested based on those which the English Tourism Council found worked well during the foot and mouth crisis.

a) Business barometer

Ideally, this should be an update on measured levels of business over a very recent period (last week/last month). Most big businesses will track their performance and will have this kind of information. In normal business conditions they will be reluctant to share this as it is information that is useful to their competitors. If you can find a way to make this generic rather than company specific, it can be shared. Those parts of the industry that are dominated by small business will be able to supply more anecdotal information, but this is still very useful. Do not be surprised if the levels of business vary widely.

b) Survival advice

There are many practical steps that a business can take to 'weather' a sudden downturn. These range from steps to protect cash flow to measures to retain staff. All the evidence is that those businesses that take action early to control their costs, recover more quickly. A simple checklist of actions to take and a list of useful contacts is very helpful to smaller businesses.

c) Government initiatives

Governments will take a variety of actions which impact on the tourism industry. These might include: general advice to the public, changes in health or security regulations, introduction of special support programmes, establishment of task forces, etc. It is good practice to brief, and keep briefing the industry on what is being done. It does not matter if a business hears about an initiative from several different sources and you should not worry about duplication in this area. It is very rare to be criticised for sharing too much information.

d) Latest research

The perceptions and fears of customers will fluctuate considerably during a crisis and it is very important to track this. It is equally important to share the research very quickly so that all businesses have the opportunity to tailor their response. This sort of research information is useful for two purposes. In the first instance it will help businesses identify when consumer sentiment is changing so that they can tailor their offers and promotional messages to be 'in tune' with the way the customer is feeling. The second purpose is that it will tell you how successful your public relations activity is and will highlight areas to focus on in the next period.

e) Advertising and promotions

This should be a round up of any cooperative campaigns. This can include all the campaign details as well as information on how to get involved. It should include response levels and booking figures if available. This section should also include examples of other regional or company campaigns that are interesting examples of good practice. The key here is to foster the view that we can all learn from each other and that new partnerships can be created from adversity.

f) Media activity & events

This section should aim to give advice about topics the media have expressed an interest in, along with background facts and figures and a suggested response. It should also summarise the level of media interest and highlight any special features which are being planned so that business has an opportunity to supply information. A calendar of key meetings is also helpful

g) Feedback

There should always be a feedback mechanism in every communication. It is also useful to probe specific topics from time to time with the aim of sharing this with the wider industry. Examples might be: standard policy on postponed holidays, Most successful promotion idea, etc.

Listening and Collecting Information

Chapter 4 looks at the question of measurement, and the information collection required to provide good quality data to business and policy makers. This section is about the skill of listening during a crisis, and the importance of being seen to listen.

I have suggested that the briefing system should always have a feedback mechanism. This is essential, but you should be aware that the level of response will generally be low. (This is true unless the lead organisation or the government does something *very* wrong, in which case you will get a big postbag.) This does not mean that people have nothing to say. In every business and organisation there will be a desire to hear from industry 'leaders', and have the opportunity to comment. People look for leadership during a crisis, and visibility is a key part of leadership. The role played by Rudolf Guiliani in New York on 11th September is a perfect illustration of this. We are not all blessed with the personal gifts of Guiliani, but you should not underestimate the positive response generated by someone who is visible and is seen to listen. This can be done by anyone, at every level in the industry – there doesn't have to be only one leader. The informal and anecdotal feedback you will get from this exchange is just as valuable as the market research data.

Speaking with One Voice

This brings us neatly to one of the biggest challenges the industry faces. When you listen to what business has to say, you will find that the picture is very varied and will change quite quickly. During SARS, inbound tourism to Australia dropped by 21% in the month of May. However, if you consulted businesses in the state of Queensland in May, they had just enjoyed a good Easter and were reporting healthy levels of business as domestic Australian customers made up for the lost international visitors.

How do you represent this complexity to the media and government in a way that is consistent and coherent? The lesson from around the world is that it works best when you have established a mechanism to agree key messages. The drafting of the key messages will be done by the public relations experts, but the adoption and use of these key messages needs to be accepted by a coordinating body. Some examples of such mechanisms are covered below.

The Tourism Cabinet

During the foot and mouth crisis, the British government enacted its normal emergency response procedure. This included the establishment of a communications centre for all government departments. The government then asked the English Tourism Council to establish a similar mechanism for the tourism industry which would act as the communication point with the government. A group was established which was called the Tourism Cabinet. This group was established by invitation and consisted of 12 individuals who could speak for all sections of the industry. Each individual gave a commitment of time and accepted the responsibility for providing feedback to their constituents. The group took an overall industry view and concentrated particularly on media messages and summarising industry views to the government.

Tourism Industry Emergency Group (TIER)

The experience gained during FMD was extremely useful and led to an agreement that a response group should be established which could be called into existence in response to any crisis. This system was tested very quickly when the group needed to be established after September 11th. The secretariat for the TIER group was provided by the British Tourist Authority and the focus of the group was on media messages. Appendix 1 contains a summary of the agreed procedures and processes.

The Tourism Alliance

In Britain 2001 was a very difficult year for tourism as the two unrelated events of foot and mouth and 9/11 hit both the domestic and international markets. The heightened interest in the industry illustrated the need for a single point of contact for the government and the media. There was a growing acceptance that this need was broader than the short-term contacts which arose as the result of a crisis, and that the industry would benefit from learning to 'speak with one voice' on many issues. This led to the establishment of an all industry body called the Tourism Alliance. The purpose of this new group was to increase the awareness and understanding of tourism across government and to lobby for change if this was necessary. It was established as a permanent body rather than a crisis response group.

Toronto Tourism Industry Community Coalition

The SARS outbreak in 2003 had a dramatic impact on business to Toronto due to the number of infected individuals and global media coverage. Tourism is Toronto's second largest industry and the major organisations resolved to work with government to address the crisis. In April 2003 it was agreed that a coalition body would be created which brought together hotels, motels, restaurants, the Board of Trade, the city authorities, State government and marketing bodies, and chaired by Tourism Toronto. This coalition set itself a remit of generating positive media coverage and drafting a recovery plan for the city. In September 2003 it was awarded substantial funds by the government of Ontario for tourism marketing.

Fiji Tourism Action Group

Fiji has experience of recovering from two periods of political instability following the coups of 1987 and 2000. In both cases, a coordinating body was set up, the Fiji Tourism Action Group (TAG). This included the Fiji Visitors Bureau, the Fiji Hotels Association, the Society of Fiji Travel Associates, the national airline, Air Pacific and the Ministry for Tourism. The TAG mobilised the Fijian tourism industry to respond rapidly and worked with inbound operators and the media to rebuild the image of Fiji as a safe place to visit.

The Eye of the Storm

Whatever the crisis, there will be a need to support tourism operators and reassure them that the crisis is being managed professionally. A coordination point that generates useful updates and listens to the feedback that is being provided by the industry can make a huge difference to the confidence level of the industry. If it is well run it will be the eye of the storm.

Measuring Impact
How Bad Is It?

Within 24 hours of some unexpected event there will be demands for an assessment of the likely impact of the event from the media and government. Observers of the tourism industry might be surprised to discover that a simple question like, 'How bad is it?' could generate so many possible answers. This chapter identifies some of the characteristics of the way tourism is measured and explains how this might influence the way organisations and governments will arrive at answers to that simple question.

Measuring Tourists

In Chapter 3 the tourism industry was described as a sector rather than an industry. A further complication is that tourism does not feature in the standard classification of economic activity used by governments, known as SIC (Standard Industrial Classification) codes. Several sub sets of the tourism industry – like hotels – do have an SIC code and some – like catering – have a code but these are partly but not wholly tourism related activities. As tourism impacts on so many other economic sectors – for example, retailing – it is very difficult to measure the total economic activity which results from tourist spending.

The significance of this is that the normal ongoing measurement of economic activity that is carried out by the government will only give a partial view of tourism as a sector. To compensate for this, countries have developed a variety of different survey methods to give a more complete picture of the health of their tourism industry. The most common means of measuring international visitors is to survey them at ports and airports using information from immigration documents or by doing a sample survey of visitors as they arrive and depart. The sample survey is the method used by the UK government, and it is called the International Passenger Survey.

This still leaves countries with the challenge of measuring domestic tourism. These visitors do not cross any national borders, and in most countries the majority of visitors travel by car so they cannot be measured by traffic through stations or airports. In economic terms, domestic tourism often earns more for a country than international tourism and therefore a good measure is very important. In the UK a customer survey is the chosen method and this is done by phone at monthly intervals looking at what trips customers have taken in the previous two months. This is known as the UK Tourism Survey.

These 'demand side' measures are those that can give the most comprehensive view of the sum total of economic activity by tourists, as tourists themselves report their expenditure on all types of activity including visits to attractions, meals out, souvenirs, etc.

Naturally, within such a big industry there are also 'supply side' measures such as the occupancy levels of hotels and the reported numbers of visitors to tourist attractions. These supply side measures are also very important but they are a snapshot of business in sub sets of the total industry. As a result of this it is possible to find yourself in a situation where different representatives of the tourism industry may appear to be making statements on the impact of a crisis that appear to contradict each other. This is highly undesirable as it leads to a loss of credibility in the industry and mixed messages in the minds of the public.

Measuring Immediate Impact

The difficulty you will face in the short term is the need to produce impact information quickly. The more comprehensive 'demand side' surveys will give a complete picture but they are not available quickly. In most countries in the world the fastest turn around time for 'demand side' surveys is between one and two months after the survey month. Just to make life even more interesting, it is quite common for the international and domestic surveys to be on a different timetable making it very difficult to produce a complete picture.

This issue tends to force countries in a crisis into using short-term measures of impact. These can be a mix of demand side and supply side measures which are robust enough to produce credible information and varied enough to be a reasonable representation of total impact.

The ideal situation is to identify what short-term measures of impact are going to be used and to commit to using these at regular intervals over a six to twelve month period. This has the advantage of providing a benchmark of performance immediately after the crisis and an opportunity to track any improvement in business more quickly.

Industry Surveys

A common sense approach to finding out information about loss of business is to ask individual businesses how much their turnover and booking/enquiry levels are down at a point in time. It is HIGHLY desirable that all those organisations that need this information agree in advance what questions need to be asked and commit to sharing the information that is obtained. If this does not happen the businesses themselves will be deluged by a variety of questionnaires which cover slightly different periods and pose slightly different questions. It is bad enough for a small business to be worried about cash flow and whether they can afford to pay the wages without having to deal with several different agencies asking how bad things are.

This is clearly an area for industry leadership and can come within the remit of whatever coordinating group has been set up. There is no ideal interval for monitoring but an initial exercise after one month should be followed up at least every three months until the end of the year.

Industry Associations
and Chambers of Commerce

A crisis can take so many forms that it may happen that different parts of the industry may be much more affected than others, e.g. bushfires may make rural tourism impossible, but increase the business that goes to coastal areas. Industry Associations will want to be active in helping and representing their members and may well wish to be proactive in measuring impact. This is good and should be encouraged as it will add to the total picture of what is going on in a complex industry. The only note of caution is that such information should always be placed in the context of the bigger picture. The coordinating group has a crucial role to play here in ensuring that this valuable and rich information gets into the public domain in a way that increases the understanding of government and the media, and does not lead to confusion. It is possible to explain that there is a mixed picture. It is much harder to explain headlines which appear to contradict each other: "Recovery under way says tourism chief"; "No sign of business returning to countryside" are two real headlines reported by one newspaper in the UK within a 24 hour period.

The second note of caution is that Industry Associations do tend to represent large and medium sized businesses that are active in their sector of tourism and this may give a skewed picture of the total impact. Small and very small businesses (which make up 80% of all tourism businesses) are often overlooked in industry surveys.

Tourist Information Centres/Visitor Centres

Many countries have an excellent network of information points for tourists and the staff in these centres regularly monitor and report on levels of business. This can be a very efficient barometer of what is happening RIGHT NOW. If this monitoring can be established very quickly and be done on line, this is likely to be the best source of fast information. These centres can also be tapped for qualitative information on the state of mind of visitors so that any anxieties can be picked up and responded to in the PR and Marketing activity. Just remember that this source is excellent but it is based on a sample of customers who have chosen to travel and it is therefore not a good source of information about future business or the anxieties of those who have chosen not to travel.

Barometer Businesses

In an ideal world a monitoring programme can be established which is comprehensive and consists of a large enough sample to be statistically reliable. In the real world, a country or destination may not have the people or money to recruit and run a large scale monitoring exercise, but will still need to know about the impact of a crisis. This where people tend to fall back on what is sometimes called 'Quick and Dirty' research. This is just a pragmatic response to a management problem. A group of tourism businesses are identified which give a reasonable spread geographically and by type of business and are asked to contribute information on a confidential basis. This information can be collated and the collective picture can be shared widely.

Consumer Information

Emergency support systems can be put in place to deal with customers concerns and provide practical information. These most commonly take the form of telephone help lines and/or websites. The use of these is covered in Chapter 8, but they are also useful as a measure of impact over time. In the first instance calls to help lines are an indication of customer anxiety and their need for up to date information. The volume of calls to help lines can often be a reverse indicator. At the start of a crisis call volumes are likely to be considerable and grow in the first week or two. As the number of calls starts to drop it can be an indicator that the immediate worries of visitors have been addressed. At this point the help line and/or website can become much more of a promotional tool and be used to measure indications of a recovery.

Lies, Damned Lies and Statistics
How bad do you want it to be?

As with all exercises involving the collection of data, it is possible to interpret information in many different ways. The many sources of information discussed earlier, demonstrates that it will be possible to get many different answers to the question "How bad is it?" It is worth thinking about some of the factors which will influence your answer.

Differential impact

Most destinations in the world receive tourists from a variety of different source markets and these tourists travel for different purposes. A major crisis is likely to have an immediate impact across all types of business but it will soon become apparent that the medium and long-term impact will vary across the country and between types of visitors. To try and understand the likely pattern of impact it helps to have a very good picture of the make up of existing business.

To illustrate this, Chart 1 gives a pictorial analysis of England which shows the reliance of different parts of the country on earnings from international visitors. This shows that London earns 70% of its tourism income from international visitors, whereas the north of England only earns 5% from international visitors. This pattern explains why two crises, occurring in the same year (2001), had a totally different impact. The Foot and Mouth crisis closed the countryside and was a headline issue for

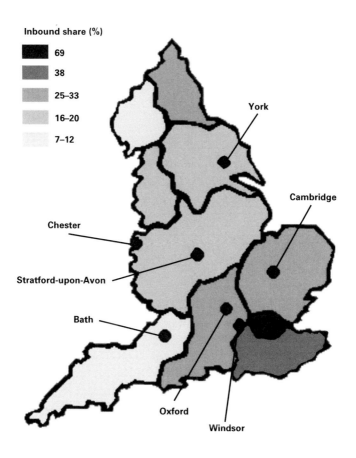

Inbound share (%)

69

38

25–33

16–20

7–12

York

Cambridge

Chester

Stratford-upon-Avon

Bath

Oxford

Windsor

Chart 1 Inbound vs. domestic spend by region
(Source: IPS and UKTS 2000)

UK residents. Those parts of the country, which were almost totally reliant on the domestic market, were very badly affected. Later in the year, the events of 11th September had a major impact on international travel. This was much more serious for London and the South East of England. So, if you were a hotelier based in London the picture would have changed considerably as the year went on. Governments are less concerned with sectoral differences and will be most interested in the total economic impact. However, they may be interested in regional differences when deciding on fiscal support packages.

Business postponed or cancelled

As tourism is a perishable product – you cannot stockpile hotel bedrooms – it might be argued that lost business is gone forever. One of the key debates in the early days of a crisis is when and whether lost business will come back. If the crisis is relatively short lived, then it may be possible to persuade customers to postpone a visit until later in the same season. This would result in occupancy levels varying significantly over the year but the net result might be that the level of business is in line with the original budget. The convention is that if business does not materialise within that year then it is treated as lost business. The issue of timing then becomes important in trying to answer the question "How bad is it?"

If an individual or business is optimistic that this is a short-term event then they may plan on a quick recovery. Many businesses anticipated that a short (less than two months) campaign in Iraq would mean that customers would postpone making plans and would delay travel until later in the year. This would mean that lost business could be won back in the same year and there was a lot of coverage of an apparent 'Baghdad Bounce' in booking levels as soon as hostilities came to an end. In practice this recovery was not sustained and business only partially recovered.

This illustrates the fact that a question addressed to companies before and immediately after the war could only produce their reading of the situation at the time. You cannot really tell if business has been postponed or cancelled until after the end of the year.

Setting a base year and opportunity cost

Most businesses set their budget based on the preceding years actual level of business and their forecast for conditions for the current year. If a crisis happens after the year has started it is possible to calculate lost business in two ways. Two simple examples illustrate how this can change the message quite considerably.

The first method is the simplest and most easily understood. The country or company reverts to the actual level of business in the preceding year and judges a gain or loss as an increase or decrease on that figure.

Example 1

	Actual Bookings	*Budget Bookings*
Last Year	100	
This Year	90	110

Calculation of Lost Business

Units Lost	10
% loss	$\dfrac{10}{100}$ = 10%

The second method starts from the assumption that there was an expected level of business that would have materialised if the crisis had not occurred. This method argues that the true loss is the difference in what would have taken place and what actually took place. This is sometimes called the 'Opportunity Cost' as it recognises the lost opportunity to grow the business over and above what had been achieved in the previous year.

Example 2

	Actual Bookings	*Budget Bookings*
Last Year	100	
This Year	90	110

Calculation of Lost Business

Units Lost	20
% loss	$\dfrac{20}{110}$ = 18%

Does it Matter?

If you are not a statistician you may not think that it matters which of these two methods companies use. It is important to think about how such information will be used and how your customers will see it.

In the short term, the media will be interested in dramatic headlines and an 18% loss looks more dramatic than a 10% loss. If
you are making a case to government for an aid package then
you may prefer to use the 18% figure as it supports the argument for special measures. If you are a private business you may
want to use the 18% figure in an insurance claim for loss of business. These are the 'Upsides' of Example 2.

The 'Downsides' are about public perception. Customers do
not want to spend their leisure time in the middle of a crisis or
in a depressed area. It is very true that customers are deterred
from going into an empty restaurant, and a similar feeling can
be created by too much doom and gloom. If your customers
believe that the quality of their holiday will be affected by the
gloomy picture being painted by the statistics than you may
damage your long- term business.

For companies that are listed on the stock market, the risk is to
the perception of the business by shareholders and the impact
this may have on the share price.

Finally, government may provide an aid package but there will
be evaluation at a later date of the case that was made for support. If the industry has been seen to over dramatise the crisis it
will lose credibility. A perception of " Crying Wolf" will not help
when the next crisis comes along.

Decisions, decisions

At the end of the day you will need to arrive at some figures
which you believe are realistic and have been researched as
much as time and resources allow. The picture will change
over time and this will be understood if you are clear about
the story you are telling. What you are trying to do is make
the complex simple and maintain the integrity and perception of the industry as mature and professional. The only
advice I can give is don't make it up – you are in this for the
long term.

Non-financial impact

In the first year of a crisis the over riding interest will be on the financial impact of a crisis and most people will talk in terms of how many millions of pounds or dollars have been lost. There are other impacts which may not be apparent until year 2 or 3 but are worth thinking about early because of the possible effects on business.

Investment

A loss of business leads to a loss of profitability and this will often lead to a reduction in planned levels of investment. If this means that a new project is postponed until business levels recover, then this is the operation of normal market forces. If this means that existing businesses delay or cancel refurbishment or planned improvements, then this could be very serious for the recovery of the industry. There is ample evidence that customers' expectations increase every year. A delay in refurbishment or planned improvements effectively means that your product standards will not be keeping up with the competition.

It is useful to be aware of this as it is an issue to consider when briefing financial institutions or government agencies. Many governments are not well disposed to making compensation payments to tourism businesses after a crisis, but they are more sympathetic to fiscal incentives for investment. This sort of business case can highlight the double benefit of such investment. Any money spent will be recycled through the community as expenditure on materials and payments to tradesmen. It will also allow tourism businesses to maintain high standards which will help to avoid a cycle of decline.

Quality

One of the longer term risks to the health of the tourism industry after a crisis is a possible drop in quality. This can arise because of a lack of investment, as mentioned in the preceding paragraph or for a number of other reasons. One of the most widely used marketing tools, both during and after a crisis, is price reductions. This can be very effective for kick starting a market that has collapsed but it does carry some risks. Many customers like a bargain but they do have expectations of a country or brand that have been developed over time. It is quite common for customers to expect that a drop in price will not mean a drop in service and if they are disappointed they will be lost as a customer in the future.

This is a dilemma which is very familiar to marketing professionals and each business will decide on the level of risk it is comfortable with. Many businesses are more comfortable with the idea of added value and Chapter 8 explores this.

A third reason for a drop in quality is the risk that trained staff could not be retained during the downturn and businesses go through a phase of retraining when business picks up again. Most businesses will do everything they can to keep good staff and it is worth exploring with government mechanisms to keep people in employment to avoid this problem.

Customer satisfaction surveys are a very important tool and can be used to track a gradual drop in the customers' perception of the quality of their experience. It is worth thinking about adding a few specific questions to the standard surveys for two to three years after the crisis to ensure that this risk is monitored.

Business failure rates

In the first month of a crisis the doom and gloom merchants will be making predictions about how many businesses will not survive the downturn. The hard headed economists will argue that this is just a version of natural selection and only the strong will survive – so the industry may emerge in better shape in the long run. Tourism is a peculiar industry that does not always conform to economic theory. It is a fact that many tourism businesses are 'lifestyle' businesses where the main asset is also the business owners home. Typically, these people do not look for commercial rates of return on their investment and are not free to realise their main asset without becoming homeless. These lifestyle businesses may not be carrying significant debt whereas the forward-looking companies who are investing in product improvement may well be carrying a debt burden. Darwin's theories may not apply and the strongest may not survive.

After the first Gulf War in 1991 an attempt was made to look at business failures in tourism. It is true that a record number of hotels went into receivership in the UK in the mid 90's. The general conclusion was that the major influence on this was the economic recession and that the war had only a minor impact. It is also true that many of these companies did not cease to exist, they just changed ownership.

Tracking business failure rates in tourism is extremely difficult. In countries where there is no statutory registration required before a business can operate there is no complete register of who is trading in any one year. In any year a proportion of businesses fail and are replaced by new entrepreneurs and this dynamic marketplace is normal. This is only an issue for countries who are thinking long term as a drop in supply of hotels might limit the ability of the market to grow in the future. It might also be an issue if one type of product was disproportionately affected by a crisis. An example might be the loss of rural bed and breakfast accommodation in a country whose major selling point was rural tourism.

The opportunity to think about these issues at the start of a crisis is useful because it will promote a debate about possible undesirable impacts and allow the industry and government to take steps to prevent problems and protect the long-term health of the industry.

Conclusion

Tourism is a very significant industry and contributes hugely to the economic health of many countries. A good understanding of how and why the industry is likely to be affected by any crisis and the ability to quantify this impact is important for business and for government. This chapter has looked at how to monitor and measure impact and given suggestions for tools you can use. Chapter 9 looks at the issue of forecasting and the influences on speed of recovery. These two issues are closely connected but measuring impact tends to be more backward looking and recovery more forward looking. To be most effective you will need to think about both.

CHAPTER 5

Yes Minister

All of the types of crisis outlined in Chapter 1 will involve action by government. In this chapter the term government is taken to be inclusive and covers local, national and, sometimes, international action.

The Role of Government

Any significant event will attract the interest of government. In the first instance their concern will be for the safety and security of citizens and the restoration of infrastructure, followed by decisions on remedial action. Tourism is a casualty of a crisis but is likely to be considered only after any life threatening issues have been dealt with. However, any government will be aware of the economic importance of tourism and will be keen to see the industry recover. In the last few years of crisis, governments have intervened in a variety of ways and this chapter looks at some examples of this intervention.

General Crisis Management Measures

Every country will have mechanisms for responding to a crisis which will operate at local or national level. The general practice is that a small group will be created to focus exclusively on the issue and will have a senior politician in the Chair. This group will be decision making and will manage communication across government (local and/or national). The issue is treated as high priority and specialist support and advice is sourced. In Britain a national level crisis triggers the establishment of a group known colloquially as a 'War Cabinet'. The event will trigger the establishment of a Civil Contingencies Committee, sometimes called COBRA – apparently derived from Cabinet Office Briefing Room where the Committee meets.

Whatever the mechanism, it is very important that this group is well briefed on the tourism industry and that a means for quick confidential consultation is established when possible actions are being discussed. This avoids a decision being taken which may solve one problem but create a different problem for tourism. The trickiest area here is in relation to terrorism and security. No government will want to cut corners on its security measures, but the way these measures are communicated may intimidate citizens and potential visitors. There is no glib answer to this. All that can reasonably be asked is that those in authority think about the broad impact of any measure.

Chapter 3 examined the benefits of having an industry communications group to speak directly to government. This can act as a very quick channel of views and can be the liaison point for the government committee. You should not assume that Ministers or advisers understand the tourism industry and you will need to be prepared to do a lot of briefing.

Chapter 6 reviews key messages and the importance of nominating a messenger appropriate to the message. In the first stage of a crisis the government will have instructions for citizens and visitors and it is right that such messages are delivered directly by the government. At a later stage the messages are about re-establishing the destination and therefore the messages should come from marketing bodies (endorsed by politicians if appropriate).

Your objective should be to establish a partnership with government and its agencies to enable informed decisions and mutual benefit.

Government Measures Which can Support a Tourism Recovery

There is a multitude of ways in which government can intervene to support the tourism industry in a crisis. One of the difficulties is in knowing which support measures are most helpful in the circumstances – and therefore what to ask for. During the foot and mouth crisis a range of measures were put in place and they were assessed after the event to establish how valuable (or not) they had been.

Foot and mouth business support measures

The foot and mouth epidemic had its most dramatic impact in the countryside and the majority of tourism businesses that were affected were small or medium sized enterprises. This meant that a special emphasis was placed on remedial measures that would be of use to small businesses.

a) **Offers of training/retraining of staff.**
Special exemption was given to staff that were laid off by their employer which allowed them to receive training without this affecting their entitlement to state benefits.

b) **One off grants to individual businesses for promotions expenditure.**
Small grants (£1,000) were allocated to businesses for promotions expenditure after the completion of a simple application form.

c) **Free consultancy from financial advisers.**
The Small Business Service provided free business consultancy advice to companies in financial difficulties.

d) **Deferral of payment of taxes and VAT.**
The Inland Revenue allowed businesses to defer

payments for a period of up to a year if the business was able to demonstrate hardship and/or a drop in business.

e) **Reduction in business rates.**
    Local authorities were given financial support by the national government to offer up to a 90% reduction in business rates to those rural businesses that could demonstrate hardship.

f) **Government loans with beneficial terms.**
    The Small Firms Loan Guarantee Scheme was extended to allow businesses to borrow with a government guarantee.

g) **Subsidy of fees or free membership of tourist boards.**
    Membership of tourist boards gave some automatic marketing benefits to the business. The annual fee was either discounted or waived.

h) **Subsidy of fees for quality inspections.**
    Accommodation businesses in the UK need an annual inspection to ensure their star rating is assessed and the property is eligible for the Quality promotion scheme. The fee for this inspection was either discounted or waived.

i) **Funding to establish consumer information help lines or extend their service to 24 hours.**
    Most parts of the country had tourist information services but these were restricted to office hours. This funding enabled the hours to be extended and a national help line to be established.

j) **Funding for promotions campaigns.**
    This funding was usually allocated to a designated lead body within an area, which then created a marketing campaign which smaller businesses could

participate in.

k)   **Match funding to charities that provided rural support services.**
     Many news organisations were sympathetic to the plight of farmers and established appeals which generated donations from the public. The Treasury agreed to match fund these contributions on a £ for £ basis. Farmers and rural businesses could then apply to the charity for assistance.

l)   **Grant aid for businesses which invested money in product improvement.**
     Many businesses were cautious about spending money on upgrading or maintaining their property as they had not made a profit for the year. Limited financial support was provided in some parts of the country.

m)   **Financial support for business development..**
     Businesses could bid for development funds if they could produce a business plan which was felt to enhance the tourism product in the area.

Most of these measures were agreed nationally and financed by additional support from the government. However, they were implemented on a regional basis and therefore the range of support measures available did vary.

What did we learn from this?

Several forests have been felled to produce detailed evaluation of each of these measures. Rather than repeat the exercise it might be more useful to look at what was most helpful. The overwhelming message from most businesses was that their immediate problem was lack of cash. Therefore any measure which provided cash or allowed them to defer making payments was appreciated. This was particularly true if the paperwork was simple and the business did not have to prepare complex business plans or produce accounts for several previous years. As most tourism businesses are small and entrepreneurial, they have little patience for form filling and a mistrust of bureaucracy.

The next set of measures which worked were those which focussed on getting customers back. So, any promotions or marketing activity which was made possible by the allocation of core funding was popular. The key thing was having a sum of money available to start the process and develop campaign ideas. Businesses were able to work within this campaign framework and could add a financial contribution if they chose. Also, a subsidy for an existing marketing expense (like the cost of a quality inspection) was appreciated as it was easy to administer and to understand.

The loan packages on offer were not useful in the short term. Most businesses preferred to negotiate an overdraft rather than taking on a long term commitment in a period of uncertainty. Business advice was also felt to be of limited use in the short term but more useful as the crisis started to recede.

The watchword on all of this was flexibility. Businesses wanted quick decisions, understanding and minimal paperwork. The challenge for the government was to make these funds available in a way which protected against fraudulent claims. There was a great deal of criticism about excessive paperwork and long delays in getting funds to the businesses. Any measures which are simple and can be implemented quickly should be the priority.

A Recovery Package

If possible it is better for the tourism industry to prepare and agree a package of measures which can be presented to the government as an integrated set of solutions. This is likely to include short, medium and long-term measures and an estimate of the likely costs.

If a coordinating body has been created this can be used as the mechanism for the industry to work co operatively so that money will not be wasted and the customer will not be confused. The government will need an accountable body to take responsibility for the management and use of any additional public funds. The marketing element of a financial package like this is usually executed by the Tourist Board and managed by the coordinating body. It is very undesirable for the government to try and manage this marketing exercise; it is entirely reasonable to set targets and then expect the tourism professionals to make it happen. What government can most usefully do is to nominate a lead agency and be clear about the targets that are set.

Government Ministers can give support in many other ways. Hosting receptions, opening prestige government buildings for key events, welcoming VIP visitors in person, endorsing advertising campaigns, selling the country on overseas visits and taking their own holidays in the country; these are some of the ways that politicians can show real support for the industry.

The Attitude of the Government to Tourism

As one of the fastest growing industries in the world, tourism is now taken seriously in most countries. Its contribution to GDP and the jobs it can create has led to tourism enjoying greater seniority in the portfolio of responsibilities within government. There is, however, quite a range of attitudes in evidence, with a laissez faire approach in some countries to interventionist policies being pursued in others. In countries like Dubai and Egypt, tourism is at the top of the political agenda. In the US and Western Europe, a much more laissez faire approach is sometimes found. This is important to bear in mind when making a case for government support. Some governments – and the UK government is one of these – believe that tourism is a profitable and successful industry which should not need government intervention. This means that they will question the case for providing public funds for support and start from the assumption that the industry should help itself.

Making the Case for Government Support

If the coordinating body decides to make a proposal to government for financial support for a package of recovery measures, it will need to prepare a business case. An assessment of the economic impact of the crisis will be the foundation for the business case. There are also some tests which may be applied by government economists to check whether there is a need to invest public money. It is useful to be aware of these when putting any proposal together.

Market failure

Naturally, any government is wary of demands for more public money to be spent. One of the tests that is often applied is to look at whether there is 'market failure'. Market failure examines why the normal market mechanisms might not work – and therefore why there may be a case for spending public money. An example of a market failure argument is on skills and training. It could be argued that it does not make sense for a single business to invest in training its staff as they may take their new skills to another employer. The economy as a whole will benefit from having a more skilled workforce but the individual business may be disadvantaged. This is why public money is allocated to fund the development of skills in the population.

In tourism terms this argument is often applied to the issue of expenditure on marketing a destination. If a single hotel spends money on advertising London then the hotel may benefit but so will other London businesses and the economy of London as a whole. This means the cost is borne by a single business, but the benefit is enjoyed by many and this is inefficient. This 'market failure' argument is the most common justification for allocating public money to the promotion of a destination.

Displacement spending

You should also be aware that economists will examine the case for any support for tourism by looking at the economy in the round. An example of this was the debate that took place during the Foot and Mouth crisis on 'displacement spending'. When making the case that rural businesses were suffering as a result of a lack of UK visitors, government economists wanted to examine the overall spending in the economy. The logic was that if UK residents were choosing to spend their money in hardware shops in cities, rather than in a rural pub, then the total economy was not adversely affected. There are many counter arguments that can be advanced which highlight the extent to which tourism expenditure is recycled and has other benefits, such as sustaining rural businesses. The general point is that you will be dealing with people who do not automatically hold the view that tourism is 'A Good Thing' and must be sustained.

Return on Investment (ROI)

Any business will track its return on investment by looking at the profit achieved as a result of the investment. The challenge for the tourism economy is to find a way to measure ROI as profit is achieved by many players as a result of a range of investment decisions. Several countries have tried to track the ROI achieved by destination promotions by tracking the behaviour of the customer. The general principle is to monitor the responses to an advertising campaign and then through follow up research among visitors isolate how much additional expenditure was generated as a result of the advertising campaign. This amount is then compared with the cost of the advertising campaign to give a ratio. This methodology was used by the British Tourist Authority over a number of years and an ROI of 27:1 was generally quoted. There are flaws in this methodology and it is by no means accepted by economists – but it is a start. The key thing to remember for your business case is that you will be asked to demonstrate the effectiveness of any public investment. The marketing team need to be aware of the measurement requirements before they start planning a campaign – and not afterwards.

Winning support

It is quite common to find that a regional or local body will be much more receptive to arguments about the economic benefits that flow from tourism. Their frustration is that they do not often have the resources to provide financial assistance. Nevertheless, local government representatives can be powerful allies and supporters of tourism and should be fully involved in any business case that is made to government.

It is important to make use of your communications network to explain the package of proposals to the industry as well as to government. It will help the credibility of your bid enormously if the industry is seen to be united and supportive of the proposals.

Political Reality

At the end of this chapter it is worth reflecting on the fact that business and government are different. While everyone will start with a desire for the crisis event to be managed properly, a government will also be acutely aware that its performance is being judged and its capacity to manage this crisis will affect how it is seen generally. Timing will also be very important. If the crisis comes close to a key event like a local or national election, you should expect everything to be seen through that prism. There will inevitably be tensions if the government wants to say that everything is getting better when the tourism industry believes that there is only a faltering recovery. You will have to strike your own balance on issues like this.

You should also accept that the government machine has its own way of working. It may seem peculiar, but in a crisis you don't have time to change it. Government officials don't like surprises and they like everything written down. A fast decision is one that is made in less than two weeks and there may not appear to be any logic to the process of decision-making.

It is a good idea to use the post crisis period to review how well government and industry worked together and to agree any changes to the process of communication before the next crisis hits.

CHAPTER 6
'They Would Say That,
Wouldn't They?'

One of the most powerful, perhaps *the* most powerful, weapon in your armoury during a crisis is Public Relations activity. A crisis has an impact on all areas of the business and so activity is required on a broad front. However, the one area where you cannot afford to fail is in Public Relations. The existence of multiple media channels and 24-hour coverage of news places huge demands on organisations at the centre of a news story. Getting PR activity right is not enough on its own, but if you get it wrong it makes all your other activity much less effective.

The second thing to bear in mind is that PR and Marketing activity are intimately connected and an integrated approach is essential if you are going to maximise the results you achieve by your efforts. In the first few weeks the PR activity will be most visible. As the crisis progresses the balance will change so that the emphasis moves to marketing or re-launching the destination. PR and Marketing are covered as two separate topics in chapters 6&8 but these two activities should be seen as two sides of the same coin.

The Messenger

Chapter 5 has reviewed the role of government and touched on the issue of news management. Any event that can be called a crisis will be a major concern of the government. In most crises, the event itself needs management and this will involve the emergency services and support from local authorities. In most cases tourism suffers as a secondary consequence of an event e.g. an oil spill on a beach kills fish and birds but deters tourists. The significance of this in PR terms is that the government will have messages for the public which are to do with their safety and security. They will want the public to take these messages seriously and to pay attention to any special instructions. They will also want to convey an image of confidence and competence to reassure citizens.

In the short term this is totally appropriate. The main messages need to be government led and the input from the tourist industry should be very factual. Tourism is a huge industry and it will be affected by a crisis, but while people may be in shock or mourning loss of life it would be callous and insensitive to focus on business.

As the 'news' element diminishes and the public start to come to terms with the event there is then a hunger for a wider range of information. At this point the secondary effects of an event will become much more newsworthy and this is the point when there will be huge demands for information about tourism from the media. At this point those who are going to speak for the tourism industry need to be briefed and ready. The timing of this will depend on the scale of the crisis but it will be between a day and a week after the original event, so there is a limited time to prepare. The steps to follow are covered in the section on the 'Emergency Phase'.

Once the scale of the event and its consequences are better understood there will be a need to stabilise the situation. For tourism interests this means protecting as much business as possible in the short term, and persuading the public to stick with their plans and not cancel their bookings. This second phase, the 'Reassurance Phase', is where the debate about who the messenger should be may get interesting. In most parts of the world we are dealing with a sceptical public who have become used to filtering advertising messages. In Europe this manifests itself as a degree of suspicion about the motives of the messenger – hence the chapter title 'They would say that, wouldn't they?' Some ideas on how best to frame messages during this period are covered in the section on the 'Reassurance Phase'. This still leaves you with the tricky question of who should deliver this message.

During the foot and mouth crisis in the UK, the English Tourism Council commissioned some research on the perceived trustworthiness of a variety of messengers. This showed that the more personal the experience of the messenger, the greater credence was given to the message. It was also true that if the messenger was seen to have an 'agenda', i.e. if the messenger would benefit in some way from the message being believed, the public tended to be sceptical. The third useful message was that tourism authorities were seen as having more credibility than politicians. How you break this news to politicians is up to you!

What is clear is that it is difficult, if not impossible, to contain a message about security and precautions alongside a message of reassurance. In England local councils erected signs along footpaths to indicate that the footpaths were closed due to disease. At the same time, the government was placing advertising which encouraged people to visit the countryside. The result was that the public were left with a fear of 'doing the wrong thing'. All of the tracking research showed that the public believed that the right thing to do was to stay away from the countryside and it took a lot of time and effort to persuade them to a different conclusion.

There will always be an uneasy compromise in this area when you are trying to balance risk, security and loss of business. While you cannot be entirely black and white about it, it is worth agreeing at the start that government will take a lead on safety and security information – what you can't do- and tourist boards should take a lead on travel and tourism information – what you can do. If the relationship works well there should be a gradual change of emphasis from government led to tourism led information and PR.

Since 9/11 there has been a greater focus on terrorism related security advice. While some parts of the world have had a to live with a reputation for being 'high risk' destinations, the difference is that this is now seen as a global problem. It is now a much bigger consideration when customers are planning their travel. There is ongoing tension between the travel industry and governments about the security advice given to travellers   (known as travel advisories). These are important as they give an official view of the risks involved in travel to a country, but they also affect the ability of customers to get insurance cover. In 2004, some governments have recognised the need to adjust their advice and have made a commitment to identify more precisely the area of risk, rather than giving blanket advice about a whole country. This is designed, in part, to help the tourism industry. It is important to be aware of the travel advice that is being given about your destination and to make representations to the appropriate government if it is not accurate.

An End to the Crisis

In this section we have been debating the issue of who delivers messages during the crisis. One of the final sensitive areas is the question of who decides when a crisis is over. This will not be an issue in every situation as there will be a gradual return to normality in many cases. However, where there is a health threat, the decision on the end of the crisis is very significant. It is extremely helpful if there is an independent third party that can speak with authority. The role of the World Health Organisation in the SARS outbreak is an excellent example of a body that was intimately involved with the crisis and was able to give a reasoned and independent view that had immediate credibility. When the WHO said the disease had been contained, the public accepted that information. An environmental body could play the same role if the issue was one of pollution.

In the UK, the announcement that Foot and Mouth disease had been brought under control was made by the Prime Minister, supported by government scientists. This announcement was made in May 2001 and the last outbreak of the disease occurred in

September 2001. The British public treated this announcement with some scepticism, as they were aware that an election campaign was due to start (and had been delayed as a result of this crisis). The Prime Minister was reluctant to call an election until the disease had been brought under control and therefore there was a perceived benefit to the government of declaring the crisis over. There was no obvious independent agency that could have played the same role as the WHO, but if there had been it would have made the message management much easier. As it was, it was a struggle to convince a sceptical public that things were improving and the tourism recovery from Foot and Mouth in England was more gradual than the recovery from SARS in Hong Kong.

Once the crisis is over (however this is defined) it is time to start the fight to get business back. This is the 'Promotion Phase' and here there is little debate that the messages should be led and managed by tourism organisations.

Organising a Communications Hub

PR teams usually have a focus on media relationships but there will be a significant demand for information from the tourism industry. During normal business conditions many organisations separate their trade relations and media relations functions, but it may be worth bringing these activities together during a crisis. The ideal is to create a communications hub where information can be collated, packaged and disseminated for different audiences. Chapter 3 outlined some possible content for trade briefings. Most of this material would also be of interest to the press but it may need condensing and editing. Even if you do have specialists, there are real benefits to be gained from co locating the individuals and encouraging the constant exchange of information as the situation develops.

Working with the Industry

Chapter 3 provided some examples of coordinating bodies set

up by the tourism industry in order to cope with a crisis. The single most important thing that such a body can achieve is to ensure that consistent and coherent messages are delivered to the world. If the group is to achieve this it will need a lot of support and advice from the PR team in message management. At each stage of the crisis appropriate PR messages will need to be developed that will be supported and endorsed by the industry group. This does add another layer of complexity to the PR job but it will be more effective.

Key PR Tasks for Each Stage of the Crisis

The 'Emergency' Phase

Initial Response
In the very early days of a crisis the greatest demand from news organisations will be for factual statements and background briefings. Many reporters will be coming to the story with little existing knowledge and they will want to understand the issues very quickly. The focus will be very much on the story as a news item and they will be looking for dramatic headlines. This presents an immediate challenge as the answers journalists are looking for may simply not be available. It is best to recognise that you are an expert in your industry and a background briefing which is based on properly researched data combined with some early estimates of impact will help the journalist to meet deadlines and establish your organisation as a credible source for briefing purposes. This is important as you will want to build up a relationship with the news media so that you have an opportunity to influence the style of coverage as the crisis progresses.

Chapter 3 has explored the idea of setting up an industry co-ordination group. If a group already exists it will have procedures for operating in 'crisis' mode. The agenda for this first meeting needs to be about media messages and the aim should be to agree on a set of statements and facts and figures which all players in the industry will use. This consistency of early messages is very important as it will build credibility and start the process of setting the agenda for later coverage. It is quite natural that different sectors within tourism may wish to emphasise how their particular part of the business has been affected. This is helpful and gives variety to the media coverage as long as it is set within the context of the broad facts and figures being used by everyone.

Another issue to settle very quickly is the question of one or more people who will speak on behalf of the industry to the media. These individuals should be selected from those who have had training and are experienced enough to convey a professional image. Journalists will always seek out their own sources and look for an original angle on a story so they will not always work with those who are suggested to them, but they are working under time pressure and are more likely to use someone who is available and well briefed if they are offered.

This first briefing will need to cover the common sense questions:

☞   What has happened?
☞   What does it mean for visitors?
☞   How many visitors normally come to XXX and what is that worth?
☞   How many visitors will stay away/cancel?
☞   How much business will be lost and how much revenue does that mean?
☞   Where can visitors get information?
☞   How long before conditions return to normal?

This sort of information will be what is required for the first few days or up to a week. Once the initial shock has subsided the demands will change and become more varied and complex.

Providing Material to Your Own Employees
Most travel companies need to deal with global media interest and will get demand for information 24 hours a day. While you may have a policy that limits contact with the media to nominated individuals, you should assume that all staff may be con-

tacted for information. As part of your marketing activity you will also be compiling information to help your staff answer detailed questions from customers (Chapter 8). This is likely to be more detailed and specific than a journalist would want but there needs to be consistency between the messages. The most common and useful PR tool for staff is the Question and Answer brief. This is a format that most people find easy to use and the process of drafting the brief helps to identify gaps in your knowledge and issues which may be sensitive.

In most organisations the Q&A document is not intended as a publication that is given to the media, but more a prompt sheet for those who need to answer questions. You do not need to be over sensitive but it is wise to assume that any document you prepare – even if it is for internal use – may well end up in the hands of a journalist.

At this stage you will also need to think about the question of ongoing updating of your staff and how you are going to collate market intelligence from them. Your existing systems may be sufficient or you may need to create tools like an extranet. The ideal is to create a single point where information can be shared with confidentiality and speed.

Misinformation and Rebuttals

In every crisis there will be some scare stories that will need to be dealt with. Some of these come from misinformation or a genuine misunderstanding and some will be pure fantasy. When preparing your Q&A it is worth taking some time to brainstorm as many questions as you can think of and then compiling fact based responses to them. The sillier stories will die quite quickly but some misconceptions will linger and these will need to form part of your reassurance and rebuttal activity in the next phase. As an example, many Americans believed that Foot and Mouth disease was connected to BSE ('mad cow' disease) and that they needed to bring their own food to Britain as it was not safe to eat local food. Such perceptions can quickly become received wisdom and it takes continuous effort to challenge these ideas.

The 'Reassurance' Phase

Once the initial shock has subsided, all the players will have a better understanding of the nature of the event and some of its potential consequences. You will still be dealing with a large degree of uncertainty as the trajectory of the crisis and its end point will be unknown. What you can do is to assemble good quality information, update it continuously and ensure that a quick response is provided as there are new developments or media scare stories. This is a very busy period for the PR team and they need to have excellent contact via the Marketing team with the customers, via the Management team with the government and directly with the media.

Generating Information for the Media

It is likely that the crisis will still be a big news story and there will be considerable media interest. The challenge for journalists is to find new things to say about a story in an environment of 24-hour output and media competition. Your role should be to provide balanced, fact-based information which will help to give the public a better understanding of the situation. The types of information you can use are:

1. Information from your sales team on what customers are concerned about.
2. Information from your research team on the latest consumer surveys.
3. Information from your overseas markets about how the situation is being reported and the impact this is having on business.
4. The latest statistics on visitor numbers.
5. Industry surveys on impact/ cancellations etc.
6. Measures introduced by the government to help the industry.
7. Latest updates on what is open/closed.
8. Latest advice for travellers.
9. Helplines/Websites for potential visitors.
10. How the industry is responding to the crisis.

There is a real opportunity to work with the media to help get your message across to the public but it needs to be managed professionally. Some of the ways in which you can do this are set out below.

Interviews

Your organisation, or even you personally, will get asked for interviews. Even experienced professionals can be seduced by the 'glamour' of being on national television and will want to say yes to requests for interviews. If you are going to build up a good rapport with the news media you will need to be responsive and available, but you must never forget to ask yourself the standard questions

☞   Who is the audience?

☞   What is my message to them?

☞   Is this a good opportunity or my ego at work?

☞   What angle will the journalist take?

☞   Am I the best person to do this interview?

The message should be consistent with the key messages agreed by the industry coordination group and your experiences should be shared with this group.

Press Releases

Press Releases can be very effective at getting a consistent message out to a broad audience. A release is most appropriate when you have some newsworthy information. This is either something which is new – latest statistics, something surprising – an unexpected upsurge in business, something topical – what special events are planned for the coming holiday weekend, etc. The release needs to be supported by more detailed information and one or more individuals who will make themselves available for interview. The decision to issue a press release should be made in the context of the bigger picture of how the crisis is being reported. You need to be sure that your press release is going to move the coverage in the general direction you want, i.e. a better informed and reassured public.

Media Briefing

A media briefing can be written or face-to-face and both have their uses. In a crisis the journalists are trying to understand the industry quickly and appreciate the chance to ask questions. If you have the resources to organise a background briefing in the early stages of the Reassurance phase this is likely to be very helpful. In this environment the purpose is to spend more time explaining some of the background issues to the media, so that their reporting can be more informed. In general journalists are very bright people who want to get to the key issues quickly. Good quality charts and headline information is much better received than an hour of detail. This should be followed by plenty of time for questions and the chance to have one to one conversations. All of those who attend will be looking for something to report but they will want their own angle on the story and you need to accept this.

Human interest stories

One of the ways in which a crisis can be made more relevant to a broad audience is to show how it has impacted on individuals. For the tourism industry this will take the form of stories of family businesses who have lost custom as a result of the crisis, and may lose their livelihood. Journalists may ask tourism organisations to identify such people and get their co-operation to give an interview. This can make for coverage with significant impact but as with all media approaches it needs to be thought through. The biggest risk is in relation to the timing of the piece. The average viewer will have sympathy if the interviewee is genuine and the loss is in context. A piece about lost business after an oil spill may be appropriate within days of the event. If the incident was terrorism related and involved loss of life, then such coverage is not appropriate for some considerable time.

Media monitoring and rebuttals

If it is possible and you can afford it then media monitoring will help you to understand how the crisis is being reported. More importantly, it will give you an early warning of myths and scare stories so that you can be proactive in your rebuttals. The best

way to deal with these occurrences is to assemble factual information and to be calm in your response. This does not mean
that you should be passive. Rebuttal activity is very important
and you should challenge unfair and inaccurate reporting vigor-
ously, but information is always better than indignation when
you are dealing with the media.

Video news releases

One of the ways in which you can influence broadcast coverage
is to create and make available a Video News Release. As you are
the editor of this material you have control over the tone and
style of footage, and, by making it easy for the broadcast media,
you are increasing the chances of the material being used.
Specialist agencies will create a VNR for you and therefore you
need to think about the tone and content before they start. Some
media outlets will use a VNR in its entirety but most will use
shorter extracts or just background footage from it. This is not
a cheap option but it can get you visibility around the world.

Journalist visits

A very powerful tool that you can use is to invite the media to
visit and see for themselves what can be enjoyed in the 'crisis'
area. Most industry operators will cooperate in such an exercise
by contributing empty hotel rooms or flight seats which will
minimise the cost. The benefit of such support is that it demonstrates that the industry is working together and being proactive.
There will often be some time lag between the visit and the coverage so this should not be seen as a quick fix. However, it will
generate editorial coverage which is a very powerful endorsement of the destination.

Positive stories

One of the frustrations that is often expressed with the media is
that they will not report good news stories. This is not entirely
true but it is the case that bad news sells more newspapers than
good news. As the crisis fades you may well have more good
news to report but you will find that the news journalists have
moved on to the next item. Broadly speaking, good news stories
are more likely to be taken up by feature writers or lifestyle pro-

grammes and so you need to cultivate a different set of contacts. If you have been helpful to the news media they may return the favour by pointing you in the right direction or making introductions and this will ease your path.

If the Reassurance Phase has gone well you will be dealing with more and more good news and the air of crisis will be fading. The marketing efforts to protect business should be starting to generate results and the public should be much more aware of what they can do if they are planning a visit. At some point it will be decided that the crisis is over. This is just the beginning of the next phase for the tourism industry.

The 'Promotion Phase'

The key characteristic of this phase is that everyone is now focussed on getting business back and their thoughts are turned to the future. At this point the most visible work will be done by the Marketing team, but Public Relations activity is still a critical part of the package. Most of the tools used during the Reassurance phase are still available but the environment will be less news driven and more focussed on promotional support. The mix of activity will vary but it is likely to include some of these elements.

Themes
Following 9/11 and Foot and Mouth disease in Britain in 2001, the Queen celebrated her Golden Jubilee in 2002. This was developed as a promotional theme for all activity. The Public relations elements included journalist itineraries with a 'royal' interest, researching stories about royal links with overseas countries and highlighting special exhibitions with the focus on the Royal family. This approach can be used by any destination as part of relaunch activities.

Welcome
When visitors have been deterred from visiting it is very important to make a special effort when they return. The elements can

include welcome points at ports and airports, welcome packs in hotels, welcome gifts in shops and at attractions etc. The PR role is to get coverage about this when customers are considering a visit, as its purpose is to reinforce the message that the country is back to normal.

Special offers

Most operators in the travel and tourism industry will be keen to offer incentives to visitors to encourage them to return. Some will opt for reduced prices but most will try and package 'added value' offers such as 2 nights for the price of one. The role of PR is to spread the message about these offers and to direct the customer to sources of information and booking channels.

Special events

Most major events are planned many years ahead so a focus on events is likely to be as a result of branding a major event as part of a theme, or the collation of several smaller events as part of a welcome back. The PR role is to generate a sense of urgency and to reinforce the message that these events are special and time limited to encourage wavering customers to book.

The Promotion phase is much more like normal business operations as the PR team will be a part of the marketing effort. The main differences will come from the fact that additional resources may well have been made available to try and get business back more quickly and this will put pressure on the team. The other difference is that the industry and the media will be watching to see how the hard work of PR and marketing is managed and to measure the results. It is an opportunity to prove the value of PR and is a challenge that should be enjoyed.

CHAPTER **7**

The Customer

Every customer is different, but what may help organisations to respond to a crisis is to see some patterns in the way customers behave. This chapter offers a model of the process customers will go through in reacting to an unexpected event. It is deliberately simple and will need to be interpreted for your circumstances and your geography.

The Cycle of Reaction

The last few years have given travel agents and tour operators many opportunities to track what customers do in a crisis situation. In its simplest form there are three stages which can be observed. These are Paralysis, Exploration and Renewal. These steps are similar to the well publicised change models that psychiatrists and counsellors have been working with for some time. I am suggesting that all customers will go through these stages but the speed at which they will operate will depend on the scale of the shock and the geographical distance from the country affected.

Paralysis

A world event, like September 11th, is so dramatic that the only customers who will make any plans in the short term are those who have to make a decision. These are people who are directly affected because they have a commitment to travel in the immediate future, or are en route. In these first few days, these customers will be very worried and active in making alternative arrangements. Airlines, travel agents and tour operators are well versed in the procedures to follow and most have a clear policy of making alternative arrangements or accepting cancellations.

For all other customers the shock of a terrorist event will dominate their thinking. For a period, decisions will be put on hold as people reflect on bigger issues. At its extreme this reaction is similar to the way people feel when they experience the death of someone close. It is a phenomenon that will be recognised by the Spanish after Madrid, by New Yorkers after September 11th, and by Australians after the Bali bomb. Those that do not feel so personally affected will not have such an extreme reaction. The last thing on a customers mind at this point is their holiday plans.

One of the features of this state of mind is that people will want to be with, and protect, their families and friends. It was very clear, after September 11th that a lot of people wanted to withdraw to their 'cocoon'. This was their home, their parents home or somewhere where they felt safe and could be with people they loved.

While the reaction to other crisis events is less extreme, it is still an emotional reaction and there are many similar characteristics. During the foot and mouth outbreak in Britain, research showed that potential visitors would not go to the countryside as they found the death of animals a shocking and upsetting sight. The SARS outbreak resulted in scenes of whole cities full of people wearing face-masks conjuring up images of a modern day plague. During an oil spill the emotional impact comes from the sight of fish and birds dying on beaches.

At this stage the key thing to understand is that your customers are in shock and the only thing you can offer is very good quality factual information that is easily accessible. It is too soon to start talking about reassurance, as the scale of the problem is not likely to be understood in the first week or two.

It is also likely that forward business will drop dramatically as business travel is postponed and leisure travellers suspend decision making.

This period of paralysis will last for between one and three weeks. After this point, the need for a sense of normality, exhaustion with the emotional impact of news coverage and the desire for escape, will combine to get customers focussing on normal life and thinking about their holiday and travel plans again. Customers are still very fragile and minor events can dent their confidence.

Exploration

In most countries the crisis will have united the travel industry and it is quite common for state or national governments to allocate additional funds to be spent on promotions activity. At the start of this period there is a great deal of 'common purpose'. Everyone wants to get the customers back and there is a great deal of cooperation between companies that would normally compete.

The characteristics of this Exploration period in the minds of the customer is that the 'aftershock' is still very real and the crisis event may still be playing out, for example: oil being washed up on a beach, cases of infection still being reported, etc. There will still be significant media interest and customers will be receiving some misinformation.

However, the pressure on people to get on with their plans, will bring customers back into the marketplace. There will be an expectation that there will be special offers and customers who are bargain hunters may be triggered to act if the offer is special enough.

For most customers this is the time when reassurance is critical. Tourist organisations play a very important part in providing this reassurance as they are seen as more independent than other sources. It is sometimes tempting to paint a very positive picture, but it is very, very important to keep faith with your customers. An honest appraisal of the situation, which accentuates the positive is what you are aiming for. It is important to remember that a customer who is making an enquiry wants to have a holiday and wants to be reassured. They will expect you to sell to them, but they will be unforgiving if you lie to them.

Customer Motivations

There are very different motivations at play during this period. The bargain hunter may be very dismissive of any perceived security or health threat and will just focus on the deal. There will be some trading up, i.e. a customer who would have booked a three star hotel will book a five star hotel because they can afford it within their budget. This will have a double impact on the bottom line as the revenue earned from the room is less and there is evidence to suggest that these customers do not use the bars and restaurants to the same extent as the usual customer base. There will be some people who bring a trip forward or take the opportunity for a treat, which would be beyond their means at normal prices. This will all be welcome business, but it is a different customer base and businesses will need to be flexible to make sure that these 'first time visitors' have a wonderful time. In this period of uncertainty the aim should be to turn any customer into an advocate. Word of mouth recommendation is very powerful at any time, but it is even more important when people are nervous.

Some customers will be concerned about the practical impact of any crisis and will be worried about the extent to which it may restrict their enjoyment. It is useful to think in terms of 'taster' breaks to tempt people back to your business or area. Flexibility is the key. If restaurants and visitor attractions are quiet, can local residents be tempted to become tourists in their own town? If overseas visitors are staying away can the home population be tempted with a one or two night packages? We all know how off putting an empty restaurant can be. To entice customers you need customers and so the strategy should be to kick-start the process by getting people travelling again.

It may be worth thinking in terms of the 'investment' that any visitor makes in visiting your business or destination. The decision to visit represents a commitment of time, and money; so a two-day short break is a much smaller investment than a two-week long haul holiday. There is a clear relationship between the speed of recovery of travel patterns and the scale of investment that the customer is making, i.e. the greater the investment of time and money – the slower the recovery. Therefore, local business, which involves a customer making a day trip, will recover much faster than business from long haul markets.

Customers also make decisions based on perceived risk. If a market is highly risk averse, then it will take longer to be sufficiently reassured to make the commitment to visit.

At this stage of 'Exploration' it is wise to concentrate your marketing efforts on those who are making a modest investment. Adopting this approach has several benefits. You are asking the customer to take a small risk and so your chance of persuading them is greater. You are also making propositions to the customer which do not require a lot of forward planning and so can be an impulse purchase. This means that some customers will travel at short notice which generates cash flow to businesses, keeps staff in employment and starts the process of word of mouth recommendation. Your aim is to create a virtuous circle of activity which helps everyone to start to return to a normal pattern of operation.

The issue which is the most difficult to deal with in this period of exploration by the customer is the emotional reaction to the crisis event. Many potential customers will struggle with feelings of guilt about the idea of visiting somewhere to have a good time, when the local area is still suffering. However, consumers are very aware that local businesses benefit from tourism and it is possible to emphasise the positive contribution that their visit can make to the restoration of an area which has been traumatised.

The pattern of business in this period is likely to be irregular. Business will build and then falter – especially if a news item reinforces the message that the crisis is still not over. This might be the result of a new outbreak of disease, a security scare or some other development which reminds people of their original reaction to the crisis. This will ease over time and a new set of world events will shift the focus of the media. As the story drops down the news agenda, customers will be willing to make a bigger investment in a holiday. As their confidence builds, your aim should be to have innovative packages, which are for a longer duration and welcome their return.

One of the greatest challenges in tourism is finding a way to track what is happening in the minds of customers and being able to respond quickly. This is much more critical during a period of uncertainty. Tourist Boards can fill this gap by having regular research in place which can be shared with all businesses. This issue is explored in more detail in Chapter 4.

It is also important to be aware of other events that would be having an impact on customers motivations. What is the economic data telling you? Have exchange rates moved? Are there any parts of the world that perceive themselves as unaffected by the situation? An example of this would be business from Argentina into Britain during the Foot & Mouth crisis. As foot and mouth disease was endemic in cattle in Argentina, it was felt to be a non-issue for visitors from Argentina, and visitor numbers did not suffer. Every cloud has a silver lining.

This period of 'exploration' is characterised by customers being cautious and needing a lot of reassurance or a price incentive to encourage them to travel. It generally lasts about 3 months, although it is greatly affected by when the crisis is perceived as being over. A precise ending to a crisis can often be identified and may well be 'announced' e.g the WHO statement confirming that the SARS outbreak had been contained. You should not make the mistake of thinking that the customer will accept such a statement and will need no further reassurance. Consumers have become very well informed and quite cynical about official messages and will look for independent advice. You should also be cautious about early evidence of a 'bounce' in bookings just after a good news announcement. The industry will welcome evidence of a return of consumer confidence and all good news should be celebrated. Privately, a calm appraisal is needed to see if this is a short term 'catch up' effect due to pent up demand from customers who postponed their bookings. You will need to be realistic about the work required to give customers the confidence and motivation to come back to your destination.

Renewal for the Customer – Recovery for the Industry

The third phase is described as 'renewal' as it represents the point at which the customer rediscovers their enthusiasm for the destination, but recognises that some attitudes may have changed. A question to explore is whether the crisis has fundamentally changed the customers' perception of your destination. It is highly likely that your mix of markets will be different and your marketing strategy will need to be re-thought.

It is often quoted that it takes three years for a country to get business back to the level it was at before any crisis. This is such a general statement that it probably hides as much as it reveals but it is worth accepting this time frame to examine how customers might react over a three year period.

There are as many customer types as there are customers, but for the purposes of illustration, this section summarises some common reactions.

Back to Normal

This is typified by a customer who has a strong loyalty to the destination and is probably a regular visitor. They will have a connection with the destination which overrides any concerns. This may have friends and family in the destination, a passion for something about the country (history, food, shopping, etc.), or a business interest. These customers will respond well to offers and can be enticed to visit in the first year of the renewal phase.

Bargain Hunters

These customers will have been aware of the crisis and may

respond to offers during the Exploration stage. For some, the destination will have been on their 'wish list' of places to visit and they will make a trip they could not otherwise afford. For others, they may have been before and have a mindset that says they will re visit some day. If the bargain price is really exceptional, some customers will buy without knowing much about the destination at all. In the UK, the low cost airlines responded to the period after 11th September by offering flights to continental Europe at extremely low prices. Some customers bought these flights without even knowing which country they were flying to. As offers are generally only available during the first year, then this business will be a short term phenomenon.

Do the Right Thing

After a trauma there will be a time when it is seen as socially responsible to return to a destination so that e.g. 'the terrorists don't win'. This was a significant feature in New York after 9/11, in Bali after the bomb and in the English countryside after the Foot & Mouth crisis. This provides an additional motivation for people who were well disposed to the destination before the crisis. It will only come in to play if the destination is seen as an innocent casualty of bigger events. Hong Kong and Canada benefited from a sympathetic attitude following SARS, but China did not. This reaction can be very powerful in generating business if the destination rewards this loyalty and acknowledges the customers mindset. The phenomenon will be quite short lived and will only influence customers significantly in the first year.

Never Thought of it Before

The old adage says that there is 'no such thing as bad publicity'. I can't agree with that statement but I have witnessed the effect of saturation media coverage on consumers' awareness of a destination. There will be a new audience who become aware of the region or country as a result of the crisis. These potential visitors will be awakened to the destination but still need to be sold to. They are likely to respond to image advertising and can become loyal customers. This business can start to flow to the destination in the first year but is more likely to build from year two onwards.

Always Wanted to Go
These customers are different to the bargain hunters in that they see the destination as a dream or desired place to visit. They are likely to be more security conscious and will want reassurance that it is safe to visit. They will be triggered to visit by an emotional reaction. This could be a feeling that 'life is too short' to postpone dreams following a terrorist act. The level of reassurance required means that these customers will visit from year two onwards.

These types illustrate that there is business to be won in the new 'post crisis' world. A much tougher challenge is to acknowledge the fact that some customers will be lost for the foreseeable future. This question is one for each destination following a brutally honest appraisal of its core selling proposition and good research on its customers. This need not be a defeatist process. We are in a renewal phase and it is better to be selective when reviewing the marketing strategy.

> *'High growth companies succeed by identifying and meeting the needs of certain kinds of customer, not all customers, for special kinds of products and services, not all products or services. Business academics call this market segmentation. Entrepreneurs call it common sense.'*
> Clifford & Kavanagh

What Segments are Less Attractive?

The test will be the motivation of the potential visitor in relation to the crisis.

If it is an environmental crisis, then customers who visit for peace, quiet, clean air, open spaces and 'escape' will be the hardest to win back. Later on, if you have a good story to tell about the clean up operation, they can be targeted.

If it is a health related scare, then families, older people who may be less resistant to infection and educational groups will be the most difficult to sell to. Parents will often be blasé about risks to themselves, but will not put their family at risk.

If it is a crime related crisis (murders, looting, riots) then tour operators will be wary of legal action against them, and all 'conservative' customers will be difficult to persuade.

If it is a terrorism related crisis it is the hardest one to predict. Sadly, as terrorism becomes more widespread, more customers are discounting it as an issue. It is true that US citizens were very traumatised by September 11th and this loss of confidence depressed overseas travel. Three years on, in 2004, there are signs that the US outbound travel market is just recovering. In contrast, the bombs in Madrid appear to have had a very short-lived effect on travel to Spain. It seems that European visitors to Spain do not perceive it as a more risky destination after the bombs and business to Madrid was recovering within a month. It is too early to say if this pattern will hold true for the whole of Spain. In Bali, the tourism industry is still struggling to reassure customers two years after their terrorist attacks. This means that countries will have to adopt a tailored approach and there should be modest expectations of visitor numbers.

A New World

Countries that have been through a significant event will often look back and measure impact on the basis of how long it takes to get earnings from tourism back to pre crisis levels.

The reality is that a different market is created as a result of a crisis. It is natural for businesses to want to have some benchmarks against which they can compare their business performance. It should be remembered that measures of financial performance are only part of the picture and do not represent how customers are affected.

The renewal phase is a real opportunity to win new customers, providing countries recognise that they may have to let go of some old friends in the process. Countries that recognise this have an opportunity to become stronger tourism destinations.

CHAPTER 8
Marketing Your Way
Out of a Crisis

Classic marketing is described as identifying and meeting customer needs and expectations. The question this raises is, is this any different in a crisis? My view is that the fundamentals of marketing do not change but the environment in which you are planning marketing activity is more complex.

When selling destinations, it is always the case that an individual operator does not have total control over the customers' experience, as the hotel or visitor attraction is only one part of the destination offer. Most tourism businesses have become adept at operating as a brand within a 'nest' of broader brand propositions. So a hotel in the Lake District may have its own brand ' My Hotel' which is within a region marketed as 'The Lake District' which sits within a country brand which is 'England'. The diagram illustrates the fact that, in normal circumstances, an individual business will give priority in both marketing message and money to the individual business brand 'My Hotel'. However, they will emphasise the fact that 'My Hotel' is in the Lake District and will give some time and effort to emphasising the benefits of the Lake District.

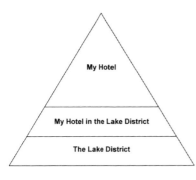

Normal balance of marketing message and marketing budget

In normal business conditions the majority of your marketing budget will be spent on promoting your brand and a small amount of the budget will support the region, country or international brand.

In a crisis it is very likely that broad geographical descriptions will be quoted to describe the area affected by the crisis. So, the media will use terms like 'the SARS outbreak in China', 'the oil spill in northern Spain', 'forest fires in the South of France' etc. This will have an immediate impact on potential customers, as they will understand that the whole of a geographical area is affected by – even blighted by – the crisis. This means that the starting point for any marketing activity has to be broader than at the level of an individual brand. The marketing messages will need to be designed to address any negative perceptions that potential customers have gathered about the area or region before you can sell your own business brand. This has the effect of changing the balance of your marketing message and means that there is real benefit in working with other businesses on partnership activities.

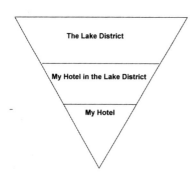

Crisis balance of marketing message and marketing budget

While this chapter has a focus on marketing, I am treating marketing and sales as linked activities. In the volatile environment you will be dealing with it is very important that marketing, sales and reservations work closely together. The sales and reservations staff are a key point of contact with the customer and will be able to provide vital market intelligence to the marketing team. They will also be able to protect your existing business if you equip them with the information they need.

The key issue in using sales and marketing to rebuild confidence and win back customers after a crisis is to ensure that the tools and messages being used are appropriate and timely.

The 'Emergency' Phase

Cancellations

The first concern of any business will be to establish whether there is any threat to the health and safety of existing customers or staff. Assuming that this has been dealt with, the next set of questions to deal with will relate to business in the very near future, i.e. the next 7–10 days. The marketing and sales team will need to review the policy on refunds in the event of cancellation and put in place a system for offering substitute holidays or alternative dates to customers. Insurance companies will also need to be consulted to establish what attitude they will take to claims in the event of cancellation.

In many ways, a very clear set of circumstances that makes travel impossible is easier to deal with in the short term. A travel advisory from the government warning against travel means that operators will automatically look for substitutes and the insurance companies will make refunds. All customers are treated in the same way and there is little room for a sense of grievance.

It is much more likely that the situation will not be so black and white and some aspects of a holiday will be affected by the event – limited access to beaches, inability to walk on footpaths, fears about becoming infected. Customers may well feel that their holiday will be marred by this and may want to cancel. This puts businesses in a tricky position, as they may have to carry the cost of any refunds and lost business without being able to make an insurance claim. Even if there is a clear policy on cancellations and refunds it may not cover an unexpected crisis. By far the best option is to offer the customer the opportunity to postpone their holiday or, for tour operators, the opportunity to select an alternative destination. This keeps the cash in the business and maximises the chance of keeping satisfied customers.

Collating information

At this very early stage, the most urgent requirement is for good, up to date information. Those customers that have already booked will be much more confident about sticking to their plans if they can be given accurate information about what the impact is like on the ground. The best way to convey this detailed information is to find a way to connect the local business with the customer. If you are a small business that deals directly with your customers, then you have the advantage of direct contact. You will still need a system for collating information on what is open and closed in the area and you will need to keep this up to date. If you are a regional or national business, you will need to collect information and make it available to your sales and reservations staff. A Question and Answer document will have been created as part of the PR effort and this can also be used, with more detail, by the sales team.

There will be a real sense of urgency about all of your activities as you try and respond on a variety of fronts. In your rush to look after your customers it is very easy to duplicate activity and waste effort. All of the tourism businesses in the area will be coping with the same problems and there is huge benefit to be gained from coordinating your efforts. This is where the industry coordination group can play a very valuable part. It is much more sensible to agree that one organisation will collate general information and make it available to all. The ideal situation is to agree that a regional or national tourist organisation will collate the information and distribute it via the destination website or internet/extranet.

A 'common sense' list of questions might include:

☞   What is open/closed?
☞   Are any activities restricted due to the crisis, e.g. access to beaches?
☞   Are there any health risks?
☞   What alternative options are there? (activities/ accommodation/transport)
☞   Is event XXX still going to happen?

These questions need to be reviewed frequently as the answers will change over time. This is why an electronic method of communication is highly desirable as it allows for real time updating. Electronic methods will only be really efficient if the majority of tourism businesses have the ability to access and update information. This is a problem that will diminish over time, but at present few countries have all their tourism businesses connected. At a time of crisis though, businesses do collaborate and exercise ingenuity.

For example, during the Foot & Mouth crisis there was a period when new outbreaks were occurring every day and this affected access to footpaths and resulted in some businesses being forced to close as they were in an infected area. The Tourist Information Network needed to be totally up to date with the latest information but was not on line. Collaboration resulted in local hotels downloading information, printing it out and delivering it to the TIC by hand. Not a 21st century method by any means – but it was effective.

Help lines

The activities discussed above are all those which can be done within and between travel and tourism businesses. The purpose of this frenetic activity is to ensure that your customers understand the situation and are reassured by the quality of the information available to them. The objective is to encourage them to continue with their trip, if this is possible, or if not, to postpone and be impressed with the company and the service it has offered in difficult circumstances.

In many cases, front line contact with the customer will fall to the sales and reservations staff. These people are experienced in customer service and have the tools to support them in their task. Quite often, though, a crisis will generate huge short-term demand for information and there is a need for a support service. Occasionally, no system exists for dealing with tourism enquiries about a whole area and it may be decided to set up a help line for a short period.

There are some advantages to establishing a dedicated help line. The number can be promoted by all businesses as a 'one stop shop', the volume of calls to the number can be monitored which will indicate the level of anxiety felt by the public, the team can be briefed to probe with specific questions which may help the planning of later promotions. Many companies offer a service which can be put in place within 24 hours and which can be flexible to cater for unknown levels of demand.

It is also worth thinking through the disadvantages of bringing in a support service. Most commercial companies that offer help line services have staff that are well trained in dealing with the public. However, they will not have detailed knowledge about the destination and its products. This problem is usually dealt with by the company asking the 'buyer' of the service to produce scripts which the telephone support staff can use. They will also provide on screen links to all the relevant websites for the sales staff. As such a service needs to be provided quickly, there is limited time for additional training and it is likely that some customers will not be satisfied with the level of knowledge and customer service they receive. You will need to make a judgement about the situation and decide if a help line – with its inherent risks – represents better customer service than not having a contact point.

You should also be prepared for mischief making by journalists. It is quite common for journalists to ring help line numbers continuously to ask questions in the hope of getting an operator to provide some incorrect information, or an operator who is unable to answer a 'local' question. This will make for an easy headline for the journalist but may undermine the confidence of the public in the service you are providing. The only way to counter this is to warn the staff that this may happen and have an experienced operator on hand to take any unusual calls.

Websites

The company or destination website can be a very effective way of keeping people up to date and needs to be managed by the Marketing and PR team working together. In the first instance, a simple information page is sufficient which can give brief details and a referral point for further enquiries. These days the expectation is that websites will be updated very frequently so this needs to be kept under constant review. As the situation develops it may be the case that a dedicated website is required but this is part of the decision-making that will take place in later stages.

Advertising

At the start of a crisis it may be the case that there is a need to get a message across quickly to a mass audience. Taking large advertisements in the press can be organised at speed and is used quite frequently. Chapter 6 explores some of the issues to consider about the message and the messenger. It is highly likely that this first communication will be conveying information and instructions. It is essential that marketing specialists advise on how this message is constructed but it is better to position the message as coming from the government or an arm of government. It is not a good idea to try and mix messages about health and safety with messages about tourism. The marketing team should be developing some thoughts for the reassurance phase which will be a softer message. For now the message will need to be about 'telling', the opportunity for 'selling' will come later.

Planning

A key role for the marketing team is to start thinking about the future and how the situation will play out. To plan effective campaigns they will need a good understanding of how customers are reacting to the crisis. Some of this information can be gleaned from feedback from the sales staff but it is also important to think about research exercises. An omnibus survey that can track consumer perceptions at regular intervals should be commissioned and thought should be given to some in depth research through focus groups. The marketing team should also be very involved in doing some scenario planning so that they can prepare options for the type of marketing campaigns that might be appropriate.

An example of tracking research conducted by the English Tourism Council is included in Appendix 1. This shows how customers' perception of a visit to the countryside changed over time. Detailed information such as this is very useful when briefing advertising agencies.

The Reassurance Phase

By now the nature of the crisis will be broadly understood but you will not always know how long it is going to last. The marketing job to be done is to reassure the public, protect existing business and generate some short-term new business. This all needs to be done in a way which is consistent with the image of the destination and will not do long term damage to your brand or business. By now, many businesses will be facing a cash flow problem and may want to generate cash by offering cut-price deals or discounts. This is one of the weapons in your armoury but it needs to be used with care and after giving some thought to the longer term.

The marketing message

At this point it is time to make the switch from telling to selling. In the first couple of weeks the public will have been receiving messages from the government or local authorities which gave them advice or instructions about the crisis. What you need to do is a very different job. In simple terms the government message is about what people cannot or should not do. Now is your opportunity to start the process of being positive and telling people what they can do, what's good about your destination and why they should visit.

This stage is about putting together tactical campaigns which will generate business in the short term, which will be consistent with your existing brand values and will not damage your business in terms of price and position in the long term.

Being positive does not mean being in denial and pretending that everything is fine, it means putting the focus on the good news. This might include talking about what is open rather than what is closed, about special offers and special events and it should inspire a sense of urgency to encourage customers to visit immediately.

This has been called the reassurance phase but how reassuring can you be and still be credible? This is a matter of judgement but good quality information will make the job much easier. If you base your message on hard facts, e.g. 50% of tourist attractions are open, one road is blocked by floods, 8 out of 10 planned events are going ahead, then you will be seen as credible and will keep the trust of your customers. It is much more difficult if the crisis relates to terrorism or security. It is a foolish person who describes their area as 'safe' in our uncertain world. Marketing practitioners are wordsmiths and sensitive use of language is called for. So you may be able to describe a city as 'vigilant' in relation to terrorism. For many years the Northern Ireland Tourist Board used to say 'no tourist has been killed in the last 30 years in Northern Ireland' as an example of factual reassurance.

Working in partnership

Most travel and tourism organisations are experienced in working in partnership with other companies as part of the process of packaging and selling their product. In normal business conditions most partnership activity will be with non-competing product. So, a hotel group will work with a tourist board, a car hire company and an airline on an advertising campaign. The fact that most crisis events are based on geography, tends to bring bigger groups of partners together and it is quite common for these companies to be competitors.

This does present special challenges to the advertising agency as they will want to avoid producing advertising which is so bland it looks like it has been produced by a committee. For partnership activity to work it is important that a 'neutral' organisation takes the lead in bringing the partners together. This could be a Chamber of Commerce, a Tourist Board or the Department of Tourism. If the government is providing substantial funding to assist, this also makes the task easier as the body nominated to account for the funds can be the final arbiter in cases of dispute. Some basic principles need to be established before the partnership can brief any agency. In particular there should be an acceptance of the key message and brand which will be used. There should also be some thought given to how the partners can measure the effectiveness of their participation. The guiding principle should always be that the promotion must work for the target customer and be kept as simple as possible. If it can be done, avoid the 'death by logo' effect of a lot of competing logos obscuring the marketing message.

Non tourism partnerships

One of the good things about a crisis is that it brings people together and encourages a spirit of cooperation. When an area is devastated by fire or flood or some other disaster it is often the case that the corporate world will be willing to help to get the area back on its feet. For the tourism industry this means that companies that have had no previous relationship with tourism may become partners in recovery campaigns. In Britain, oil companies and supermarkets worked with tourist boards to help the countryside recover from the Foot & Mouth crisis. In other parts of the world clothing companies, banks and others have been willing participants in recovery campaigns. Marketing professionals should be flexible in the design of campaigns to allow for this sort of participation. These relationships formed in adversity can be extremely helpful in the future.

Price cuts and discounts

Most crises affect the desirability of your destination in the eyes of your customers. Business visitors may worry about delays and problems with getting around and holiday visitors may not want to spend time in an area which they see as 'troubled'. Most customers want their holiday to be an escape from the problems of the world. This means that your product has become less valuable to potential customers and they may well expect this to be reflected in the price.

Some businesses in every destination have tried price cuts and this can be a very effective short-term response. In the UK the low cost airlines responded to the 9/11 event by putting very cheap airfares in the market place and this was very successful. The difficulty for these airlines came later as the very high profile promotion of low fares led the market to expect that low price was the new benchmark price. If you are seen to cut your prices across the board then you will need to think about how you can increase them at a later date to a level that gives an acceptable return. If generating cash is what you need to do to survive then price cuts are worth considering but you may need to present it as a discount to protect future business.

As travel products are perishable, many companies have used third parties to sell their last minute spare capacity (often known as 'distressed stock'.) The early examples of this were airlines using consolidators that distributed tickets through agents known as 'bucket shops'. This allowed the airline to protect the integrity of their pricing structure but still sell seats that would otherwise be empty. In the e-business era this role has been taken on by new suppliers such as Lastminute.com, Wotif.com, Ebookers and Expedia. These outlets can be extremely effective at selling distressed stock and are building a growing loyalty in the marketplace. You will still need to think about the long term impact of this on your business – if customers can get a better price with a third party, why should they book early and deal directly with you?

Special offers and added value

An alternative to price cuts is to add more to your product

offering or to disguise price cuts as special offers. The advantage
of this is that such offers can be time limited and they do not
cannibalise your usual price structure. The disadvantage is that
they are more complex to explain to customers and therefore
they may not work as quickly or as efficiently as price cuts.
There is no limit to the ingenuity of the travel industry when it
comes to special offers and added value. Typical offerings are 2
for the price of 1, Sunday night free, children free with adults
etc. Value added offers include wine with a meal, theatre tickets,
health treatments, car rental, welcome packs, free rail travel,
bathrobes, etc.

'Taster' breaks

Your aim is to get the market moving again and build the confidence of the public so that they will invest their time and money
in your destination. It is quite natural that your customers will
be cautious about planning a visit, particularly if it involves a big
commitment of time and money. You can build confidence grad-
ually and one strategy is to tempt people back into the market
by asking for a small commitment. This could be for a lower
price than usual or a shorter time than usual. Your target market
for such 'taster' breaks are those customers who can reach your
destination with ease. A typical definition of this is customers
who can travel to your destination in three hours or less.

Loyal customers

One of the challenges you will be facing in your marketing activity is that you will be trying to counteract a bad news message
which will have been conveyed by the mass media. The situation
in your local area is often not as dramatic as the picture painted
by the nightly news. Customers who do not know the country
or area are more likely to accept the message given by the media.
Customers who have visited in the past will balance the media
interpretation with their own knowledge and information gained
from friends and local contacts. Your reassurance message needs
to go to all potential customers but it is sensible to think of tar-

geted activity for regular visitors and your loyal customers.

Specific campaigns can be mounted quickly if you have a database of previous customers. A very powerful database can be created if all the partners in a promotion agree to merge their customer data to the mutual benefit of all. Electronic campaigns can also be remarkably cost effective if you are able to target the offers to the interests of the customer.

New customers

In the short term you may have to look at generating business from markets that are not your traditional customers. In many historic cities in Europe more than 70% of visitors to cultural attractions such as museums are international visitors. Theatres and restaurants in London and New York are very dependent on 'out of towners'. It is a good idea to look at the customers on your doorstep as they may well be receptive and can respond to promotions almost instantly.

Local residents can also be great allies in getting the area back on its feet. As well as persuading them to sample their local attractions , they can become ambassadors for the area. In particular they can be encouraged to invite friends and relatives to visit and to spread the word about their good experiences of the area.

Campaign websites

Tailor made websites designed to support your tactical campaigns can be very useful as they allow you the flexibility to monitor responses and to add more special offers and deals as they are created. If you are going to develop a specialist site it is sensible to think about making the most of your investment and seeing if you can find a way to link it to or integrate it with your normal branding and promotion activity. If you do create a 'stand alone' site you may be reinforcing the impression of crisis when your aim is to move the public towards a perception that the area is getting back to normal.

Monitoring

Your campaign activity will provide a variety of measures such as initial response, web usage, bookings, calls to the help line etc. These need to be reviewed regularly along with the research information that is coming in from the consumer surveys that are being conducted. All this information will give you some guide to the mood of the public and will allow you to adjust the marketing message. As the media coverage diminishes and customers start to return it is time to start planning for the next phase.

The Recovery Phase

In most instances the trigger for the recovery phase is some confirmation that the crisis is over. Chapter 6 explored some of the sensitivities that may arise in deciding if a crisis is really over. In some circumstances there will not be an 'end', there will just be a judgement made that it is time to move on. An example of this took place in New York after 9/11. At a point when the rubble had been cleared from the Twin Towers and the memorial services were over there was a desire in the city to talk about the future and to encourage visitors to come to New York because they wanted to and not because of a need to express solidarity with the victims of terrorism.

The recovery phase is the final step in getting business back to pre crisis levels. Chapter 9 looks at recovery periods and how long it might take to achieve this. While there are many variables that will have an impact on your recovery, there is a lot of good evidence to suggest that a concerted promotion campaign will make a real difference.

Characteristics of a 'recovery' based promotion

In thinking about your options at this stage you may consider the possibility of just reverting to the advertising and promotions activity that was planned in the era before the crisis. This would have the advantage of being cost effective as the creative work would be in place. It may also reinforce the message that the area or business is getting back to normal. This is not a bad option but you may miss out on some new markets or partnerships that have developed as a result of the crisis. What you want to achieve is a promotions plan which can bridge the gap between the crisis and your enduring brand values and image.

The industry coordination group is likely to have debated the timing and style of relaunch activity and may well have made a proposal to the authorities for additional financial support to cover promotion costs for both the reassurance and recovery phase. In the last few years, many governments including those in Britain, Canada, Australia and the US, have allocated generous funds to help the travel and tourism industry get back on its feet. Such funds allow the destination to achieve much higher visibility and impact but usually need to be spent on a partnership basis and may have other special conditions. All of these factors will tend to lead to a decision to prepare a tailor made campaign for the relaunch. If you are in a position to mount a special campaign there are some features it would be useful to consider.

Creating a sense of urgency

One of the risks of large scale media coverage of a crisis in your destination is that the destination slips down the customers list of places to visit in the near future. Most customers carry around a mental 'wish list' of destinations and have some views on when they might like to visit. If your destination takes on a problem aura as a result of the crisis, the mental wish list is adjusted and your destination may drop off the list completely or it will be seen as somewhere to visit at a distant date. Media coverage about the end of the crisis is always less extensive and so customers will be left with an impression of a problem. The marketing challenge is to ensure that people receive a positive message and one that conveys a sense of urgency to encourage them to move the destination up their personal 'wish list'.

There are many ways to do this but a good example is the 'Only in Britain' campaign run by the British Tourist Authority. The campaign was funded by an additional £20m in promotional funds from the government and was run in partnership with a host of commercial organisations. The basis of the campaign was that 2002 was the year of the Golden Jubilee of Queen Elizabeth. A range of special events was already planned for 2002 and these were built on to make it a very special year to visit. Tailor made promotions material was created and special offers based on the theme of royalty were developed by the industry. The campaign had a target of generating one million more visits in 2002 than in the crisis year of 2001 and this target was achieved. It was due to chance that the Queens Jubilee year coincided with the post crisis period but this was an opportunity that presented itself and was taken advantage of. The sense of urgency was created by emphasising the fact that this was a unique opportunity to participate in the celebrations and was reiterated in the campaign tag line 'Only in Britain, only in 2002'.

Welcome

An analysis of destination advertising can be quite a depressing experience as there are a few common claims made by many different countries. One of the most frequent claims is about the friendliness of the people and the warmth of the welcome. Most countries see themselves as welcoming even if the visitor might disagree.

In the post crisis period the tourism industry will be keen to see visitors return and will be anxious to welcome them back. This can be used as the core of the marketing message in this promotion phase but it is likely to be most effective if this is a given a new or different emphasis compared to the normal destination advertising. It can also have a real impact if it relates to a place that is not normally perceived as welcoming. An example of this is New York. The adjectives that might be used to describe New York might include 'buzzing, exciting, cutting edge, 24 hour city etc'; it is not seen as a place where the residents can spare a lot of time for visitors. In this environment a campaign which emphasised the genuine desire of New Yorkers to see visitors return could work very well.

An example of a campaign based on the theme of welcome was the campaign run in England after the Foot & Mouth crisis. This crisis had led to the closure of rural footpaths and the perception that residents of the countryside wanted visitors from urban areas to stay away to avoid the risk of spreading the disease. The campaign theme was 'Your countryside, you're welcome' and was based on the involvement of hundreds of rural communities making special efforts to reach out to urban dwellers. This was accompanied by supporting material which highlighted the re opening of footpaths and emphasised the joys of walking in the countryside. The involvement of the farming community in activities designed to provide a special welcome to urban visitors was central to this campaign.

Themes and special events

Themes are a familiar marketing tool for countries. A theme might be created as a result of an anniversary, such as Australia's promotion of 1988 as Bicentenary year marking the founding of the colony in 1788. It may be triggered by the tradition of a country, such as the designation of 2005 in Britain as the 'Year of the Sea', it might be created as a result of some external recognition such as the nomination as a City of Culture. The fact that a country is hosting a major event may also lead to the development of a theme to support that event. So, when Malaysia hosted the Commonwealth Games in 1998, the year was designated a year of sport. Themes can be extremely flexible and make it easy for large and small businesses to use the overall promotional messages in their individual marketing activity.

However, both theme based promotions and special events need long lead times and take a lot of organising. Tour operators around the world like at least two years notice of such plans so that they can contract seats, tickets and accommodation and build these offers into their brochures. This does mean that you will need to be realistic about what can be achieved in the post crisis period. If you are lucky you will have some event or theme which was already in development and which can be built on to be a big part of your relaunch plans. Unless the theme is well developed it is wise to think of this as a tool that can be used in the second or third year of your recovery period. The trick for winning the customer is to develop an idea which arouses curiosity and has novelty value. The original idea must have 'legs' i.e. there must be a basis for the claims that are being made, some events to celebrate the theme and some history for those who are genuinely interested. An example might be a theme of 'Christian Heritage'. This could feature churches and cathedrals, trace the history of Christianity in the country, feature towns and villages where great Christian thinkers were born and develop some walks or trails around Christian monuments.

One of the benefits of planning for year two or three is that it gives you an opportunity for continuity in your relationships within the travel industry. The crisis will have brought people together and the fact that you have a long term plan for recovery will make it easier to keep your partnerships vibrant and positive.

Iconic figures and celebrities

One of the things you will want to achieve with your promotions plans is impact – you will have a limited budget available to counter the negative impressions given by the media. You may also want to convey credibility and offer reassurance. These two demands may lead you to consider running a promotions campaign based around a celebrity or a campaign led by a senior government figure.

If your objective is to convey authority and reassurance then a significant government figure could be asked to endorse your message. In 2002 both Tony Blair and George Bush were featured in campaigns designed to welcome back overseas visitors. In considering this as an option you will need to research the level of awareness that exists amongst your target customers. The fact that your President or Prime Minister is willing to lend his weight to the campaign will convey a message to your customers that your destination does take tourism seriously and wants visitors to come back. It is highly likely that the customer will not recognise most politicians, and therefore you need to make it clear to the customer that this is an official welcome from a representative of the country. You will also need to think about the difference between your domestic and international audiences in their attitude to representatives of government. The ideal solution is to develop a promotions package that can work with and without an endorsement, as this will give you greater flexibility.

Celebrities have huge marketing power and can be the driving force behind some global brands. This influence comes with a price tag and most destination advertising does not feature celebrity endorsement due to budget constraints. Even if budget were not an issue there would be some debate about the selection of celebrities. Most countries want to appeal to a wide cross section of visitors and there are few individual celebrities that have this international appeal as well as cachet with a broad age group. A campaign designed with celebrities in mind would probably feature several different personalities. In a post crisis period there are often celebrities who are willing to lend their support in order to get the country back on its feet and this may make a celebrity based campaign affordable and achievable. In selecting celebrities you should adopt the same disciplined approach of checking that the profile of the celebrity and your marketing message are aligned. If you are designing a campaign for a worldwide audience this is even more important.

Destination features and special offers

Offers and added value continue to be an important part of your marketing toolkit but by now you should be moving away from a cut price message and putting the emphasis on the added benefit the customer will get from a visit to your destination. Offers can support the overall campaign theme and be enhanced as feedback becomes available from the Reassurance phase. If the public relations activity has gone well you should have had a number of travel journalists visiting the destination to prepare up to date features. These features can often be expanded to larger 'Destination Specials' run by magazines and newspapers. These can be supported by one or more special offers which can be used as part of your monitoring activity.

Tracking business and 'Aftershocks'

The good news is that business will return but don't expect it to be a smooth path to recovery. As the crisis subsides the level of media coverage will drop and other issues will be at the forefront of your customers mind. Their awareness of the problem will fade quite quickly but any anxiety associated with the destination will take longer to diminish. Your positive messages delivered consistently will speed the process of building confidence. One of the things you will need to be prepared for is 'aftershocks'. Typically these are occurrences like minor outbreaks of disease some time after the all clear has been given, smaller terrorist incidents or breaches of security after a major attack, etc. These incidents will have a disproportionate effect on visitors' confidence as customers' trust is still quite fragile and business may drop again after a seemingly healthy period. When this happens you may need to revert to a greater emphasis on reassurance messages to respond to the mindset of your customers. These incidents are setbacks on the path to recovery and emphasise the importance of sustained efforts to rebuild business.

Chapter 9 looks at the issue of recovery and how a country decides that business is back to normal. Marketing is fundamental to a healthy recovery and the rebuilding of the destination – however this is measured.

CHAPTER 9
How Long Does it Take to Recover?

In the introduction to this book in Chapter 1, an attempt was made to draw some distinctions between the many different events that can be classified as a crisis. This is not just an academic exercise as there is good evidence to suggest that the public will respond in different ways to each type of crisis. This understanding can help with forecasting the likely impact of unforeseen events on business.

In many crises terrible things happen, people die, animals die, buildings are destroyed and individuals lose their livelihoods. Acknowledging that, this chapter has a focus on the economic impact of a crisis and looks particularly at the time taken for business to recover. Many countries earn 20–30% of their GDP from tourism and the loss of this income means poverty for many. It is in everyone's interest to learn from experiences around the world and work to restore a vibrant industry.

A review of tourism in the last 20 years shows that we have had many opportunities to learn about crisis management. I assumed that this experience would make it easy to forecast the path to recovery and that there would be an established formula which countries could use and apply to its own circumstances. I did not find such a formula but discovered that there was received wisdom circulating that suggested that it took, on average, 3 years to recover from a crisis. This chapter examines that assumption and suggests some refinements.

Chapter 4 did consider the definition of 'recovery' – as it can be understood in many ways. For the sake of simplicity I am taking the definition of recovery as one where business returns to the level enjoyed in the year before the crisis and this is sustained for at least two years. The purpose of monitoring recovery over a sustained period is to ensure that any short term 'bounce' in business does not distort the real picture.

The other consideration in using this definition is that it does not take any account of any underlying trend in business which was evident before the crisis. If the destination was on a growth curve, then this definition may undervalue the impact of a crisis. If business was dropping, then the crisis may be quoted as the reason for loss of business – even though some of this loss would have been experienced without the crisis. These are good points but I think that there is a lot to be said for keeping it simple.

Types of Crisis

One of the considerations in making forecasts is the issue of whether the type of crisis has an impact on the nature and speed of recovery. The evidence suggests that the same stages are gone through (emergency, reassurance, recovery); but the speed with which they are experienced will depend on the type of crisis.

Natural disasters

As a general rule tourism business returns more quickly to destinations affected by a natural disaster. Some of the influences on this are:

a)   **Scale of the disaster**
     Recovery is dependent on the restoration of the physical infrastructure and the ability of the local authorities to confirm that the area is safe. The competence of the authorities in doing this will

influence the return of business.

b) **Extent of Media Coverage**
If the story receives global media coverage, then the destination will have to work hard to counter these images when the crisis is over. There is also a potential benefit to such coverage in that it will raise the awareness of the destination for some customers and this will bring some new business in the long term.

c) **Impact on the Brand**
A natural disaster is seen as an 'Act of God and no one will be seen to be at fault. However, the way in which the disaster is handled will colour the perceptions of the destination. For example, if a Swiss ski resort was seen to be inefficient in dealing with an avalanche, it would damage the perception of Swiss ski resorts as being well organised and efficient.

d) **Point in the Season**
Some tourism destinations do get year round business, but most destinations have a season. A crisis that comes before, or at the beginning of, the season may mean that all is not lost. The immediate impact of any crisis is a drop in business of between 10% and 90% but this dramatic loss may only last for one or two months. A local disaster, like a flood, may allow a speedy recovery. For example, in the USA a flash flood in 1990 threatened the tourist season in Hot Springs Arkansas. A fast and proactive response led to a better summer season than had originally been forecast.

e) **Catchment Area of Customers**
The closer the customer base is to the affected area the greater the chance of a fast recovery. This is because it is possible to get ongoing local and

regional media coverage about the progress being made towards recovery and this builds confidence and encourages customers to return. It is also possible to appeal to the altruism of a local community and encourage them to visit to help get the destination back on its feet.

Case studies

San Francisco Earthquake
On 17th October 1989 San Francisco was struck by an earthquake which killed 62 people. Although the damage to tourism facilities was minimal, by the end of November business was down by 10–20%. A proactive promotion effort meant that business had recovered and improved by the end of 1990.

Hurricane in Hawaii
In September 1992 Hurricane Iniki hit the island of Hawaii. A 23 foot high storm surge crashed onto the southern coast of the island destroying homes, cutting power and inflicting billions of dollars of property damage. A package of financial aid meant that most of the repairs and rebuilding was complete by mid 1993. The tourism industry formed a coordinating group that designed and managed a recovery programme which ran through to 1995. Most hotels were reopened during 1993 although some chain hotels did not re open until 1994 due to prolonged insurance claims. In 1993 business started to return but it took until 1994 for a real recovery to take place.

Floods in Prague
In August 2002 severe flooding hit central Europe and caused significant damage to the city of Prague. Many hotels had to close, there was no electricity and the metro was put out of action for many months. Prague regained lost tourists quickly by identifying the areas of the city that were affected and reassuring tourists that they could still enjoy a visit. The loss of business experienced in 2002 was regained in 2003.

Conclusion

The general conclusion is that the three year rule does not apply to natural disasters and that recovery does come more quickly. Assuming that the physical infrastructure can be restored, then a destination should be optimistic and plan for a recovery within 1–2 years.

Accident/environmental or man made crisis

This group of events includes things like oil spills, smog caused by forest fires, SARS, Foot and Mouth disease, Algae bloom, etc. These events are equally unexpected but they differ from natural disasters in some significant ways.

The first difference is that the problem is prolonged and often does not have a clear end point. Earthquakes and floods are usually dramatic in their impact and take place during a short period of time. By contrast a disease may take some time to be recognised as serious and there will then be a state of crisis for weeks or months before infections cease completely.

The second difference is that there is a real, or imagined, health risk to the visitor. During a health emergency it is in everyone's interest to take all precautions and follow official guidance designed to limit the spread of any disease. The chapters on marketing have highlighted the problems of trying to combine official instructions with messages of reassurance. During the emergency phase instructions to the public must take priority and this means that reassurance activity may be delayed and this will slow the recovery.

The third difference is that there is the possibility that the cause of the crisis is man made. This will have a big impact on the media coverage as the search will start for someone to blame. The media will also look critically at the way in which the problem is managed. Both of these issues can have an impact on the customers' perception of the destination and may undermine any reassurance messages. Finally, there is often an official inquiry which will generate interest and media coverage. This usually reports at a much later date and will bring the crisis back to the public's attention. If you are very unlucky this will happen just as you plan to start your promotions activity.

Case studies

Thredbo Ski Resort Australia
In July 1997, during the ski season, there was a mudslide in Thredbo which engulfed some ski chalets. The 19 occupants of one lodge died but there was a miraculous rescue of one individual which attracted round the clock media coverage. At first the mudslide was attributed to natural causes, but as more facts emerged, it became clear that planning policies might be at fault and this led to the establishment of an enquiry. The 1997 ski season was badly affected but business did start to recover in 1998. The official inquiry did not report until 2000 and it was only then that the resort could move on.

Sea Empress Oil Spill in Wales
On 15th February 1996 the Sea Empress, bringing crude oil to Milford Haven, ran aground and released 72,000 tons of crude oil into the sea. Oil came ashore along 200km of coastline-much of it in a National Park. Part of the coast path was closed, the oil smelled and it was visible in the sea. A quick clean up operation was launched which meant that most of the oil had been removed by Easter and the water was declared safe by the end of May. A monitoring exercise concluded that the area lost £2m in tourism earnings in 1996 compared with total earnings of £160m in 1995. This small drop (1.25%) was attributed to the speed of the remedial action and the proactive promotions campaign. However, a research exercise identified the loss of some potential customers as 1 in 5 of those surveyed said that they had considered a holiday in the area and rejected it because of concerns about environmental pollution.

Foot and mouth disease in the UK and domestic tourism
At the end of February 2001 foot and mouth disease was

identified in some pigs in the north of England. This disease was no threat to human health but could be transmitted by humans on boots and shoes and was highly infectious to pigs, cows and sheep, threatening farmers' livelihoods and British agriculture. Movement restrictions were introduced for animals and all rural footpaths were closed. A huge cull of animals meant that those visiting the countryside were likely to see animals being killed and disposed of by being burned on pyres. The British public understood that the most responsible thing to do was to keep away from the countryside and as a result tourist visits dropped dramatically in the month of April.

The loss of business nationally in April was 24%, but this translated to a drop of more than 70% in some parts of the countryside. In May it was announced that the epidemic was under control but there were continuing outbreaks of disease until September 2001. Business did return quite quickly and by the end of 2001 the net loss in tourism trips was −7%. The expectation was that 2002 would be a year of recovery and there was some growth but business was still significantly down on the levels enjoyed in 2000.

The SARS outbreak in China
In February 2003 a virus named Severe Acute Respiratory Syndrome (SARS) was identified in China. This virus was transmitted by human contact and could kill. Within a few weeks cases were being reported in Canada, Singapore, Hong Kong, as well as new cases in China. One of the precautionary measures recommended was the wearing of facemasks. This reduced the chances of transmission of the disease but conveyed an image of these destinations as 'plague ridden'. New outbreaks continued for several months until July when the World Health Organisation gave an assurance that the epidemic was over. Countries at the centre of the disease, like Singapore, experienced a 70% drop in business in the month of May. By mid 2003 Singapore was predicting an end year loss of −30% of their tourism business. In practice the year ended with a loss of −19%, a better performance than had been expected.

The outbreak also affected countries in the region that had no cases of the disease. In Australia business was affected, as customers did not want to transit countries affected by the disease on their way to and from Australia. Business was down for seven consecutive months and in May 2003 Australia had a 21% drop in international arrivals. A recovery began in September and by the end of 2003 business was down by just −2%.

Conclusion

Environmental and health crises are more complex and prolonged and this will result in a slower recovery. Reassurance activity can be very effective in minimising the loss of business while the crisis is still 'live', but real recovery cannot start until the cause of the problem has been identified and dealt with. Once this happens though, business will return very quickly and destinations will experience the benefits of pent up demand from postponed trips. This phenomenon needs to be welcomed but treated with caution. The overall impact on business may not be seen for at least two years and recovery may be delayed if the crisis has damaged the 'brand'. For this category of crisis it is wise to plan a pattern of recovery of 2–4 years.

Political/terrorism

Sadly, the list of examples for this category of crisis is long and stretches back over many years. There is a difference between situations where terrorism or political instability has become part of the landscape of the country and a single incident or a war - which may be dramatic but short-lived. There are many countries where tourism has the potential to thrive, but does not, because of long running problems. Examples of this might be countries like Israel or Kashmir. These destinations are not dealing with a crisis in the usual sense, but a burden, which the people and the tourism industry must carry until a political solution can be found.

It is hard to put a value on the economic cost of this burden. One example might be Kashmir, which has suffered as a result of the political difficulties between India and Pakistan. In 1988, before these troubles, Srinagar received 722,000 visitors. By 2001 this figure had dropped to 70,000 visitors.

Another way to value the loss is to look at what happens when the political problems are resolved. In Northern Ireland peace talks led to a ceasefire in 1994 and, later, the signing of a document called the Good Friday Agreement. In the year after the ceasefire tourism grew by 20% and continued to grow – albeit at a slower pace.

The stages outlined in this book do not really apply when the problem is a long-standing one. The reality is that while long-standing political problems exist, the marketing efforts of the destination will be more like those described during the reassurance phase and will remain so until the political situation changes.

War

Gulf War 1

There have been two Gulf Wars in the last 12 years and some evidence is now emerging about the pattern of impact. The impact of the first Gulf War in 1991 has been well monitored. This war was expected following the invasion of Kuwait in August 1990 and the conflict lasted six weeks – from 17th January to 28th February 1991. In the short term the pattern of impact was an immediate, and significant, drop in business. The fact that the conflict was brief meant that it was over before the peak season for the northern hemisphere and this reduced the impact.

A look at the results for the UK showed that international visitors to the UK were down by −5% and trips abroad were down by −1.5%. One might have assumed that British residents would holiday at home instead of going overseas but the domestic market was also slightly down. This suggests that a proportion of people make the decision to postpone being away from home when there is instability. The international market recovered quickly and by 1992 international visitor numbers were better than 1990 levels.

This relatively modest shock did trigger some wider impacts: the International Leisure Group (a major UK tour operator) went into receivership and by 1994 the turnover of British travel agents was 93% of its 1990 level. By 1994 330 agents and 100 tour operators had gone out of business. It is clear that all of this could not be attributed to poor results in 1991. The fact was that Britain was going into recession in 1991 and the recession deepened through to the mid nineties. The shock of the Gulf War was not a cause of all these problems, but a poor year in 1991 undoubtedly hastened the demise of some companies.

If we try and arrive at a view on the impact of the war on tourism we can see that Britain had recovered within 2 years and the later problems were due to the economic cycle.

Gulf War 2
The second Gulf War was also brief with the 'official' conflict starting on 20th March with the bombing of Baghdad and ending on 1st May, when President Bush declared the end of major combat operations. It depressed global tourism in the first quarter of 2003, but in some countries it was complicated by the fact that they were also coping with SARS. A similar pattern of a substantial drop in business followed by a rebound (nicknamed the Baghdad Bounce by the media) was evident. Nevertheless, by the end of 2003, the World Tourism Organisation announced a 1.2% drop in global tourism – the biggest annual drop ever.

As with the first Gulf War it is a mistake to attribute all of this to the war. There were economic problems in some countries and SARS had led to lost business as described above. If we consider the Gulf War in isolation then it is reasonable to conclude that the same pattern will apply as in 1991 and this means that 2004 will be a year of recovery. This reflects the broad view of the global travel industry but there is a caveat which relates to further terrorist incidents. Confidence in travel is building but it is fragile and could suffer a setback if there are more atrocities.

Terrorist atrocities
In thinking about terrorist acts the events of 11th September 2001 stand out as qualitatively different from most in their scale and impact. The TV images traumatised a global audience but have had an enduring effect on the behaviour of Americans. International travel was affected immediately, reducing business around the globe and hitting the worlds' airlines – with one airline, Swissair ceasing to trade. By the end of 2001 world airline traffic had fallen by –2.9%. A collective marketing effort by airlines and tourist organisations, combined with security measures did reassure the travelling public and airline traffic grew by +2.7% in 2002.

However, in October 2002 there was a further incident when a bomb exploded in Bali, Indonesia. This was seen as being linked to September 11th and further dented confidence in travel. Tourism accounts for almost 50% of the Balinese economy and the impact was dramatic. In September 2002 international arrivals into Bali were 150,747 and by November this had dropped to 31,491. An attempt at shooting down a plane in Kenya and another bomb in Istanbul in 2003 ensured that the threat of terrorism was top of mind for the travelling public.

In March 2004 a further terrorist attack was experienced in Spain when a series of bombs exploded in Madrid. The reaction to this act was one of revulsion but there is some evidence to show that the impact on travel to Spain has been muted. In the weeks after the event, business to Madrid was down by 10%, but this was showing signs of recovery within weeks. Travel to the rest of Spain was relatively unaffected. Several factors may have contributed to this. The authorities in Spain were seen to have responded professionally and the police quickly arrested some suspects. The Spanish population reacted with great dignity and communicated to the outside world that they wanted life to continue as normal. The net result seems to have been that Spain is not seen as any more of a risk than anywhere else in Europe, which has neutralised the possible disincentive to travel.

The frequency of terrorist incidents has meant that the travelling public is coming to terms with terrorism as a fact of life. They are becoming more sophisticated in their assessments and therefore a standard recovery period is less likely.

Conclusion

Forecasting in this environment is extremely difficult but there are a few trends emerging. The first trend is that the desire to travel is very strong and this means that a sustained drop in trips is not likely. It is clear that the public can accommodate themselves to the fact that there are threats in the world and they will make a personal choice about the level of risk they are comfortable with. The second trend is that customers are selecting destinations with new criteria in mind. A British survey for Teletext holidays in June 2003 showed that customers had less confidence in visiting countries with a large Muslim population or where security was believed to be lax. The third trend is the long term impact of terrorism on the American public. In 2003 the USA recorded a drop of −5% in all types of tourism for the third year in succession. It will take time for US citizens to regain their confidence.

General Observations on Forecasts

Speed of the 'Bounceback'

In all of these very different situations there is a common phenomenon – and that is that business comes back remarkably quickly. It is quite clear that travellers do try and postpone a visit or delay their plans rather than cancel. This should give comfort to those businesses that go through the stress of having no customers at all for a time. This sudden spurt in business will be welcomed but it is a reflection of pent up demand and should not be taken as a sign that business is back to normal.

Predictions of doom

In the short term in most crisis situations, business will drop dramatically – sometimes by as much as 90%. In the first few weeks' destinations will try and assess the long-term impact of the crisis and they will use the evidence to hand. There are many examples of reputable consultants reviewing the evidence and extrapolating to arrive at a figure that later turns out to be an overestimate. This can be justified at the start of the process as no one can be certain how long the crisis conditions will last. It is good practice to come to a view about a range of possible impacts. It may be the case that the media will use figures from the most pessimistic scenario as that will result in more dramatic headlines. It is not unusual for those making a case for financial support from the authorities to use the 'worst case' scenario to strengthen their proposal. There is nothing wrong with either of these actions as long as the individuals who commission the impact estimates are clear about the basis for their figures and ensure that the professionalism of the industry is not put at risk by predicting doom when this is not justified.

Relentless optimism

Having spent a period of time describing how serious the crisis is for the economy, there will soon be a desire to look to the future. Most people involved in travel and tourism are natural optimists and this is reflected in their forecasts. A review of press and journal articles over the last three years shows a steady stream of predictions of recovery as being just around the corner. To be fair, there has also been a steady stream of crises to knock these forecasts. The most widely used expression in these forecasts is 'cautious optimism'. It is important to be positive but this optimism should not cloud the fact that getting business back is hard work and will take time.

Source markets

Most recovery strategies place an emphasis on rebuilding business from customers who are closer to home (In Singapore they received more Asian visitors, in Hawaii more US visitors and in the UK more European visitors). This has an impact on the volume and value of tourism as long haul visitors usually spend more per visit. The forecast should reflect the fact that a recovery in volume will probably come first and value will come later.

This review does highlight the fact that forecasting after a crisis cannot be an exact science. A consideration of the features of the crisis you are dealing with and these examples should help you to arrive at a prediction that you can explain and support.

CHAPTER 10
Looking for the Silver Lining

At the start of a crisis, the time horizon of your thinking and planning will shorten. You will be forced to focus on the immediate and urgent and will not be able to think clearly about the longer term until the situation stabilises. You will progress very quickly through the stages and will work very hard to mitigate any damage to your business and the industry. As visitors start to return and things start to improve it is understandable that most people will want to breathe a sigh of relief, take a holiday and then put the traumatic events behind them.

While this is a normal human reaction, it is also a missed opportunity. Any system is tested during a crisis and a huge amount can be learned about the strengths and weaknesses of your organisation, people and procedures. It is also a very good time for the tourism industry to reflect on lessons learned and to resolve to make changes before these lessons are forgotten. This chapter examines some common themes that have emerged out of review exercises that have taken place around the world.

A Crisis Management Process

Many commercial travel organisations have plans in place to cover business interruption and the most likely hazards that might affect their business. Events might include an accident/loss of staff/strikes/power failure/extortion etc. and good practice is that rehearsals are conducted to ensure that the plan is robust. These plans are invaluable, particularly if all elements of the business are involved in their development.

As businesses are very concerned about possible damage to their reputation, the focus of individual company plans tends to be on events which are particular to the company and over which they have control. There are many case studies covering examples like Perrier, Tylenol, Bhopal which have given crisis management specialists a core of material from which to develop good practice guides.

This book has its focus on broader crises that affect many companies and where neither the cause nor the solution is in the hands of the company. The fact that such events affect so many different types of business means that coordination is critical to success.

In an ideal world the tourism industry in a region or country will have thought through the need for a collective crisis management plan. There will also be agreement with the government on the role that different organisations will be expected to play and a process for requesting supplementary funds.

If such a plan does not exist then it is important to develop one within a couple of years of the crisis event. This crisis strategy will be more about process and communication than execution and should be developed jointly by industry and government. The advantage of doing this quickly is that it allows those that have been involved in coping with the crisis event the opportunity to input their practical experience. Chapter 3 looked at some of the industry coordination groups that were created in different countries because no formal structure existed. The plan can set out an outline structure which can be amended but which will save time being wasted on debate when quick decisions are needed.

Speaking with One Voice

This is a theme that is returned to frequently throughout this book. The reason why this issue assumes so much importance in a crisis is because we live in a world where our actions are under the media spotlight and inconsistency can quickly be portrayed as confusion or inefficiency. The tourism industry is complex and fragmented but in a crisis it needs to act like a disciplined and well-organised lobby group.

Delivering a consistent message means an enormous amount of effort needs to be put into internal communication to ensure that the hundreds of thousands of small tourism businesses support the recovery efforts and echo the key messages being presented to the media and government. It also means that work needs to be put in to build a consensus so that there is a genuine measure of agreement about the way forward.

During the foot and mouth crisis in the UK there were two main interest groups affected; farming and tourism. The farming industry was represented by the National Farmers Union, led by their President, Ben Gill. The NFU was seen to have been professional and effective at getting their message across. The tourism industry struggled with the fact that there were 4 national tourism organisations representing England, Scotland, Wales and Britain and several large industry associations. Significant efforts were made to coordinate messages but this was only partially successful and there were occasions when a different emphasis caused confusion. Many destinations will run the risk of a similar problem as a drop in business will mean that everyone affected will have an opinion. So, as an example, a problem in Sydney might be handled by the Sydney Convention Bureau, or the New South Wales Tourism Organisation, or the Australian Tourism Body. This problem can be avoided if the Crisis Management Strategy sets out the roles of the different organisations and nominates one organisation to take the lead on message management on behalf of the industry.

Diversification

Many destinations are unaware of the importance of tourism to their local economy and it is a painful shock when a crisis event means that tourists disappear. A natural response is to feel vulnerable and to debate the wisdom of being so dependent on one source of income. After the event it is good practice to review the economic strategy of the area to look at the level of dependence on tourism and the risks involved. A policy decision may be taken to diversify to a broader base of economic activity to protect against future shocks, or to diversify to a broader base of tourism markets.

London is a major tourism destination, but in 2000 it earned 70% of its tourism income from overseas visitors. As a result of this dependence on the international market, it was particularly badly affected by the events of 2001 and London hotels suffered a much greater drop in revenue than other English cities. A strategic review of tourism in London was commissioned by the London Mayor, and the review identified this as a weakness. A new emphasis was placed on growing the domestic market as a result of this review.

Many countries adopt a market segmentation approach in their marketing strategy and give priority to one or more types of customers, usually those who are high spending. One of the lessons from many of these events is that some market segments are more resilient than others. This may be on the basis of geography – US and Japanese visitors are more likely to be deterred by security concerns. It may also be on the basis of the customers' reason for making the trip. The segment known as VFR (Visiting Friends and Relatives) has shown itself to be much more knowledgeable about a destination and less likely to be deterred from travelling.

One of the lessons of any crisis is that there is no formula for responding and each event needs its own solution. It is important that the marketing team keep an open mind and actively reviews the marketing strategy during and after a crisis.

Volume Returns Before Value

Chapter 9 looked at how you define recovery and a simple

definition based on volume of visitors was used. While not a universal rule, it is very common for visitor numbers to recover more quickly than visitor expenditure. This phenomenon may be due to the fact that discounting and price cuts are an important marketing tool but it takes a long time for rates to return to pre crisis levels when price expectations have been lowered. It may also be a feature of the fact that the image of the destination has been damaged by the crisis and therefore businesses cannot charge premium prices. Finally, the business mix may well have changed as a result of the crisis with fewer long stay high spending visitors being replaced by visitors taking short breaks.

While discounts and price reductions are useful tools, it is worth reflecting on the long-term impact of these short-term decisions. Most businesses will need to do something to 'kick start' a depressed market, but it is useful to be aware that profitability will take time to be rebuilt.

Procurement

This is not a sexy topic but in a crisis you need to be able to act quickly without breaking any rules. Most crisis events will trigger some financial assistance to the tourism industry from government and this money will need to be spent in a way that complies with government accounting procedures. This means that there needs to be a fair process for bidding for contracts and an obligation to demonstrate that value for money has been achieved in purchasing decisions. For small amounts of money the normal discipline of getting competitive quotes and taking reasonable references is sufficient. It is quite likely that large amounts of money will be spent on advertising campaigns. Typically this money is routed through the public sector and needs to comply with European rules on procurement. There is a set procedure for inviting tenders for contracts with a value of more than 230,000 Euros and this process takes a minimum of 6 weeks. It is possible to apply for an exemption from this procedure on the grounds that there is an emergency situation, but you will still need to demonstrate fairness in your selection of contractors.

Governments overcome this problem by pre-selecting companies to be on a list of organisations that can be called on to deliver work in an emergency. A full and fair selection procedure is followed and then the contract remains in place for a number of years. It is a good idea to learn from the governments' experience and to carry out the same process for tourism suppliers – especially advertising agencies. You may resent the time you need to spend in selecting companies to work with knowing that you may never call on them, but it is better than trying to conduct a selection process in the middle of a crisis.

Loneliness

Much of the advice in this book is written with tourism organisations in mind. This is because tourism officers can be enablers in bringing businesses together and acting as a liaison point between government and individual businesses. Many of the businesses contacted during my research have emphasised the degree to which they feel isolated and alone during a crisis. In normal trading conditions, businesses closely guard information on performance. Sales figures are not shared openly as this would be information that might help a competitor. This pattern means that when customers stay away after a crisis, most business owners do not know whether their performance is better or worse than the norm. This can create great insecurity and damage the confidence of the small business operator.

One of the most important things that any tourism organisation can do is to recognise this as a risk and plan a mechanism that allows small businesses to network with each other. This will give the business some benchmarks to work from and will also encourage them to identify opportunities to co-operate. This will build a sense of community and enable a much faster recovery.

Flexibility

The purpose of writing this book is to enable others to be confident about what is likely to be demanded of them in managing a crisis. There are clear stages in any crisis and you can prepare for these and be ready with your plans. However, no crisis is like the last one and there is a difference between being rigid and being disciplined. Some features of every event will be unique to that event and a degree of flexibility is important.

This is particularly true in relation to your customers. Your customer contact centres or Tourist Information Centres and your research activity will help you to track the mood of your customers. Don't be afraid to bring forward or delay a planned promotion if your feedback is telling you that the mood has changed. For businesses, a degree of flexibility in your packaging or booking conditions may win you new and loyal customers. You will also have to recognise that you may not be dealing with a single crisis event. The last three years have seen a wave of crises hit the tourism industry and so you may have to abandon your planned progress to stage two and go back to stage one again several times. It may feel like a game of snakes and ladders but in the long run it will get better.

Learning to Love the Media

The travel industry generally has a benign relationship with the media. In normal times regular contact tends to be with travel journalists, feature writers and lifestyle supplements. Relationships tend to be personal, built up over time and can be characterised as symbiotic. A crisis brings the industry into contact with news journalism and it is often a bitter experience.

The only way to make this experience work for the destination is to understand the job that journalists are trying to do and seek to influence the news agenda as much as possible. It will be frustrating to see positive stories overlooked in favour of the latest sensational development, but patience and persistence will pay in the end. A professional approach to PR combined with a mechanism to build up a good contacts database will help the destination in the long term.

Remember, as you grimace at the latest sensational coverage, that somewhere in the world there are people who are being made aware of your destination for the first time. In a world of information overload, that has to be a crumb of comfort.

The Importance of Leadership

Most people will quote Rudolph Giuliani as an example of outstanding leadership in a crisis. As Mayor of New York on September 11th 2001, he was faced with an appalling situation and seemed to find the right words and the right actions immediately and in the aftermath.

Most of us do not have Guiliani's gifts, but we all have the capacity to display leadership in our own sphere. When people are honest about what it feels like to live through a crisis, the most common emotion they mention is fear. People worry about their jobs and livelihood, about how well they will manage, about their financial future and their staff. What most business operators' want is to feel that someone understands their situation and can be an advocate for them, to the media and to government. Every tourism organisation can make this happen by being proactive, showing confidence and offering reassurance to customers and businesses that the crisis will pass. A crisis can transform a community if there is good leadership. I hope this book has given you the material you need to display that leadership.

Appendix

Tier Group Emergency Response Procedure

Example of emergency	Severity
Disaster affecting travel to or within Britain, eg air crash	Extreme
Major international disaster affecting travel globally	High to Extreme
Incident within Britain that is not tourism-related but impacts on Britain's image, eg terrorism, food scare, envionmental incident	High
Localised incident that directly affects tourists, eg Swedish tourist gets attacked in Bristol	Medium to High

Response Procedures for first 24 hours depending on level of severity

1.	TIER Group member receives alert and notifies BTA Press Office	TIER Group member
2.	BTA Press Office researches and establishes facts	BTA Press Office
3.	Notify CEO/Mktg Comms Director of emergency & agree impact	BTA Head of PR
4.	Prepare holding statement & circulate to all TIER Group members, including DCMS Press Office	BTA Press Office
5.	Set up Crisis Command Centre in BTA Press Office	BTA CEO/Director
6.	Convene meeting of TIER Group[1]	BTA CEO/Director
7.	Agree the following: - impact assessment - key messages - who else needs to be involved	TIER Group

- key action points

8.	Alert/convene meeting of BTA Immediate Action Group & initiate internal communications[2]	BTA Mktg Comms Director
9.	Update & circulate holding statement/briefing materials as necessary	BTA Press Office
10.	Communication to all NTB/RTB chairmen/ CEOs + press offices	BTA Strategic Partners dept
12.	Communications to wider Government(s)	BTA Govt Relations dept
13.	Communications to industry, via BTA database and TIER Group members' databases, eg BHA members	BTA & TIER Group members
14.	Customer communications, eg statement/ advice on visitbritain, statement to overseas press/trade ptnrs	BTA Information Services & Overseas Director
15.	Monitor & reassess impact	BTA Press Office
16.	Decide next steps	BTA CEO/Director plus TIER Group

Courtesy of British Tourist Authority

Attitudes to Foot & Mouth
in the Countryside in England

Wave 11 (August 24 – August 26, 2001)

Approach and sample

This outlines the key results of a survey into attitudes to Foot & Mouth in the countryside in England conducted for the English Tourism Council.

The first ten waves of this survey were conducted over the weekends of March 30 to April 1, 6 to 8 April, 13 to 15 April, 20 to 22 April, 27 to 29 April, 4 to 6 May, 11 to 13 May, 18 to 20 May, 1 to 3 June and 15 to 17 June. After a gap of nine weeks we have conducted another wave of the survey with interviews conducted over the weekend of August 24th to 26th. Each wave of the survey was carried out by telephone by Taylor Nelson Sofres among a representative sample of approx. 1000 adults aged 16 and over in Great Britain.

Key findings

General
This survey was set up at the start of the foot and mouth crisis to look at how consumers felt about visiting the countryside. It has enabled us to successfully track these shifts in attitudes as the crisis continued and consumers were influenced by both the media and information from the government.

At the end of June when the last wave of this survey was carried out, foot and mouth was still receiving plenty of coverage in the media.

Over the summer, however, there has been little or no coverage in the national press. Without this constant reminder of foot and mouth we might have expected a positive shift in consumer attitudes – but interestingly they remain largely the same as they did at the end of June. For example:

☞   24% of consumers agree that 'most places in the countryside are closed at the moment' compared to 27% of consumers in the last survey

☞   54% of people agree that 'people should keep out of the countryside to avoid spreading foot and mouth' compared with 55% at the end of June

☞   72% of consumers agree that 'you hear different messages about the countryside, some say it's open and others say it's closed to tourists' – exactly the same percentage as at the end of June

The image of burning carcasses is obviously a difficult one for consumers to forget despite the fact that this has not been shown in the media recently.

☞   35% of people agreed that 'you could not enjoy going to the countryside because you would see the destruction and disposal of animals because of foot and mouth'. This is only down 4% since the last time the survey was carried out.

☞   32% of consumers agreed that 'I wouldn't visit the countryside because of the health risks associated with burning animal carcasses. This is up 3% since the end of June.

Despite publicity about footpaths being opened up again over a third of people (35%) agree that 'you can't go to the countryside because most of the foot paths are closed'.

There is obviously still a lot of work to be done to persuade consumers to return to the countryside. Negative attitudes are not fading away as a result of a lack of negative media coverage. In fact, it appears that consumer attitudes are more entrenched and it will require positive coverage to get them to diminish. This is particularly important in light of the new press coverage about foot and mouth over the last two days.

Tourism activity

The number of consumers who say they are intending to visit the countryside in the next month or so has increased slightly from the last time the survey was carried out.

☞   48 % of consumers say they intend to visit the English countryside in the next month or so compared with 42% at the end of June.

Breaking this down further to purpose of visit to the English countryside this shows us:

☞   31% intend to visit for a day visit (6% up compared to the survey at the end of June)

☞   15% for a short break (the same as at the end of June)

☞   9% for a holiday of 4 nights or more (2% up compared to the survey at the end of June)

Earlier waves of our survey highlighted that consumers are not taking longer holidays to the countryside – instead preferring to have a day visit or short break. This trend has not changed in the past two months.

☞   36% of consumers have visited the English countryside on a day visit over the last twelve months.

☞   20% of consumers have visited the English countryside for a short break over the last twelve months.

☞   Only 16% of consumers have visited the English countryside for a holiday of four nights or more over the last twelve months.

Consumer attitudes

From the start of the foot and mouth crisis our survey showed that consumers were confused about whether or not it was safe to visit the countryside. This was also borne out by qualitative research conducted by ETC during April and June which highlighted that, despite the message coming from the government and in the media, consumers still had concerns about visiting or taking a holiday in the countryside.

In this survey we are again seeing mixed messages and confusion about foot and mouth from consumers.

For example, 79 % of consumers agree that 'there is no problem visiting the contryside, provided that you keep away from farm animals'.

But, 65% of consumers agree that 'you should not go to any part of the country where there is foot and mouth'. This is an increase of 8% since the last time this survey was carried out and has implications for tourism in the North of England where there have been new outbreaks over the last few days.

Worryingly almost a quarter of consumers (24%) still think that most of the countryside is closed. 72% of respondents agree that "you hear different messages about the countryside, some say it's open and others say it is closed".

When asked how much of the countryside is affected by foot and mouth 48% of people believe that one-half or more of the countryside is affected.

There have been positive changes in consumer attitudes since the beginning of the crisis – but the figures show that a large number of people still have concerns about the effects of foot and mouth on the countryside. This, in turn, will be influencing their tourism decisions.

Issues

Over the course of the survey the areas mentioned below have consistently shown up in the survey as issues requiring further attention.

Despite foot and mouth receiving little press attention during the past few months the same issues for consumers come up again in our latest survey:

1. *Fears of what consumers may encounter on visits to the countryside*
   35% of respondents agree that "you could not enjoy going to the countryside because you would see the destruction and disposal of animals because of Foot and Mouth".

2. *Footpath opening*
   35% of respondents agree that "you cannot go for walks in the countryside because most of the footpaths are closed".

3. *Spreading foot and mouth*
   54% of respondents still agree that "people should keep out of the countryside to avoid spreading foot and mouth".

4. *Information*
   72% of respondents agree that "you hear different messages about the countryside, some say it is open to tourists and others say it is closed".

5. *Availability of information*
   41% of respondents agree "You cannot find what is open and closed in the countryside before you go there".

Results

Visiting the countryside

Thinking now about the countryside . . . .

In the past 12 months, have you personally visited the countryside in England?

	March 30 –April 1 (wave 1) %	June 15–17 (wave 10) %	Aug 24–26 (wave 11) %	Differences (wave 10-11) %
For a day visit	31	29	36	+7
For a short break of 1-3 nights	22	20	20	0
For a holiday of 4 nights or more	17	10	16	+6
Any of these	59	49	58	+9
None of these	41	51	42	-9
	100	100	100	

Do you intend to visit the countryside in England in the next month or so?

	April 6–8 (wave 2) %	June 15–17 (wave 10) %	Aug 24–26 (wave 11) %	Differences (wave 10-11) %
For a day visit	27	25	31	+6
For a short break of 1-3 nights	15	15	15	No change
For a holiday of 4 nights or more	11	7	9	+2
Any of these	46	42	48	+6
None of these	52	58	52	-6
	100	100	100	

How would you feel about visiting the countryside in England at the moment?

	April 6–8 (wave 2) %	June 15–17 (wave 10) %	Aug 24–26 (wave 11) %	Differences (wave 10-11) %
Happy to visit	47	65	67	+2
Fairly happy to visit	28	22	22	0
Not happy to visit	24	11	9	-2
Don't know	2	2	2	No change

Attitudes to Foot & Mouth

You may have heard about problems with Foot & Mouth disease in the countryside.

I am going to read out some statements people have made about visiting the countryside at the moment. For each statement I would like you to tell me whether you agree or disagree with it.

Statements Do you agree that ..... ?	March 30-April 1 2001 Wave 1 %	June 15–17 2001 Wave 10 %	Aug 24–26 2001 Wave 11 %	Diff % Wave 10–11
Positive statements There's no problem visiting the countryside provided that you keep away from farm animals	73	84	79	-5
Negative statements Most places in the countryside are closed at the moment	63	27	24	-3
People should keep out of the countryside to avoid spreading Foot & Mouth	67	55	54	-1
People in the countryside don't want tourists visiting at the moment	44	30	31	+1

You should not go to any part of the country where there is Foot & Mouth	69	57	65	+8
You can't find what's open and what's closed in the countryside before you go there	48	42	41	-1
You could not enjoy going to the country-side because you would see the destruction and disposal of animals because of Foot & Mouth	59	39	35	-4
It's not safe to take children into the countryside with all the Foot & Mouth	35	29	30	+1
You can't go for walks in the countryside because most of the footpaths are closed	77	45	35	-10
You hear different messages about the countryside, some say its open and others say its closed to tourists	-	72	72	0
I wouldn't visit the countryside because of the health risks associated with burning animal carcasses	-	29	32	+3

Proportion of countryside affected by Foot & Mouth

How much of the countryside in England would you say is affected by Foot & Mouth?

	March 30 –April 1 (wave 1)	June 15–17 (wave 10)	Aug 24–26 (wave 11)	Differences (wave 10-11)
	%	%	%	%
All of the countryside	5	2	3	+1
Most of the countryside	30	18	18	0
About half of the countryside	37	30	27	-3
Only a small part of the countryside	26	47	49	+2
None of the countryside	0	0	0	0
Don't know	2	3	3	0
	100	100	100	

Courtesy of English Tourism Council